INTRODUCTION TO
SPANISH POETRY

INTRODUCTION TO SPANISH POETRY

A Dual-Language Book

EDITED BY
Eugenio Florit

DOVER PUBLICATIONS, INC.
New York

Published in Canada by General Publishing Company, Ltd., 30 Lesmill Road,
Don Mills, Toronto, Ontario.

This Dover edition, first published in 1991, is an unabridged and updated
republication of the work originally published under the title *Invitation to Spanish
Poetry* by Dover Publications, Inc., New York, 1964.
This edition is also published together with a cassette entitled *Listen & Enjoy
Spanish Poetry* (ISBN: 0-486-99928-9).

The following poems in this collection are reprinted by special permission:
"Castilla" by Miguel de Unamuno, by permission of María de Unamuno.
"Primavera amarilla" by Juan Ramón Jiménez, by permission of Francisco H.-
Pinzón Jiménez and Farrar, Straus & Cudahy, Inc., publishers of the works of Juan
Ramón Jiménez in the English language.
"Como tú . . . " by León Felipe, by permission of the author.
"Muertes" by Pedro Salinas, by permission of Solita Salinas Marichal and Jaime
Salinas.
"Los nombres" by Jorge Guillén, by permission of the author.
"Romance de la luna, luna" by Federico García Lorca, by permission of New
Directions. Copyright by the Estate of Federico García Lorca.
"El visitante" by Vicente Aleixandre, by permission of the author.
"Los contadores de estrellas" by Dámaso Alonso, by permission of the author.
"Página fiel" by Emilio Prados, by permission of Cuadernos Americanos.
"Donde habite el olvido" by Luis Cernuda, by permission of the author.
"El ángel bueno" by Rafael Alberti, and "El tren de los heridos" by Miguel
Hernández, by permission of Editorial Losada, S.A.

Manufactured in the United States of America
Dover Publications, Inc., 31 East 2nd Street, Mineola, N.Y. 11501

Library of Congress Cataloging-in-Publication Data

Invitation to Spanish poetry.
    Introduction to Spanish poetry / edited by Eugenio Florit. — Dover ed.
        p.   cm. — (A Dual-language book)
    Previously published as: Invitation to Spanish poetry.
    ISBN 0-486-26712-1
    1. Spanish poetry—Translations into English. 2. English poetry—
Translations from Spanish. 3. Spanish poetry—History and criticism.
4. Poets, Spanish—Biography. 5. Spanish poetry. I. Florit, Eugenio,
1903– . II. Title. III. Series.
PQ6176.I68   1991
861.008—dc20   90-23241
                                                                        CIP

Contents

vii

Introduction

Spanish poetry, according to the British Hispanist E. Allison Peers, is distinguished by three predominant traits: its energy, its idealism, and its universality. Its energy, shown in the power and directness of its speech and in an ever-renewed creativity, may be seen even in periods like the eighteenth century which seem hardly favorable to poetry. Such energy may appear in a long poem, as in "El Cristo de Velázquez" (The Christ of Velázquez) by Miguel de Unamuno, or in a *copla* or short popular song, where three or four lines express an intense idea; but it is always present, whether in medieval epics, the ballads, or the works of those magnificent mystic poets whose thought rises with the force of an arrow.

Idealism, too, sets Spanish poetry apart. While Spanish poetry, like all poetry, is rooted in the real and never loses contact with reality, it is also distinguished by unique flights of idealism, whether it is celebrating human love with Garcilaso de la Vega, or divine love with San Juan de la Cruz, or exalting some aspect of nature, liberty, solitude, or death.

It is its idealism which in turn makes Spanish poetry universal, since the more idealistic a poet's thoughts, the more universal they will appear. Concepts of love, liberty, death can be stated in any language and always seem new. By dealing with them for centuries Spanish poetry has built up almost a mythology of such feelings that will reach any reader at any time or place. In the words of A. F. G. Bell: "The Spanish genius seems to have a special gift for cutting away the accidental growths and irrelevancies which separate the individual from the universal, and the transient from the permanent."

From the first, Spanish poetry has represented an interplay between two traditions: the world of popular culture, of folklore and songs invented or sung by the people, and the world of literature, with artistic forms that are the product of literary scholars. At times the popular influence has been predominant; at times cultural influence has predominated; but both have always been present. Sometimes both currents are blended in a single poet, as in Lope de Vega; even in a poet like Juan Ramón Jiménez, in whose work the cultural tradition is stronger, the popular tradition is not absent. This double current can also be seen in the *Romancero*, a collection of ballads. Popular in origin, the ballads became ornate in the sixteenth century with the symbolism of cultured poetry, and it is with both characteristics that they have come to our own time, as in the famous *Romancero gitano* (Gypsy Ballads) by García Lorca. It is not without reason that Jiménez called the ballad the "river of Spanish poetry."

The earliest Castilian poetry we know—and we cannot take account here of poetry written in Spain but in other languages, such as Galician or Catalan—dates from the first half of the eleventh century, with the appearance, about 1040 A.D., of short popular songs called *jarchas*. Usually anonymous, or written by Arab or Hebrew poets in primitive Castilian with the inclusion of some Arabic words, these songs were later incorporated into Arab poems. Only recently discovered, the *jarchas* prove the existence of lyric poetry on the Spanish peninsula about one hundred years before the oldest of the *canciones de gesta* (epic poems), the *Cantar de Mío Cid* (1140 A.D.). By the middle of the thirteenth century a more sophisticated poetry had appeared, the *mester de clerecía* (office of clerics), with its four-line stanzas of alexandrines, a style that was to continue into the next century. It was in this style that the long religious poems of the earliest-known Spanish poet, Gonzalo de Berceo (1197?–1264?), were to appear, as well as the most famous of all Spanish medieval poems, the *Libro de buen amor* (Book of Good Love), by Juan Ruiz, the Archpriest of Hita.

In the fifteenth century the popular tradition was continued in the ballads, then beginning to be published, while the cultural tendency was exhibited in love poetry of Provençal origin, allegorical or doctrinal works, and in the *Cancioneros*, the first anthologies gathered by several poets or scholars. The influence of the Italian Renaissance was apparent at this time, as in the sonnets of the Marqués de Santillana, and there was a tendency to idealize nature and country life, a tendency becoming more pronounced in two poets of the next century, Juan Boscán and Garcilaso de la Vega. These poets, particularly the latter, are responsible for the adoption by Spanish poets of the Italian hendecasyllabic line in addition to the more traditional Spanish octosyllabic line. Together with Italian verse forms came also such Renaissance influences as the ideas of Platonism and the idealization of love, all of it reaching its height in the Golden Century, a period extending from the middle of the sixteenth to the end of the seventeenth centuries and including such diverse work as the meditative poetry of Fray Luis de León, the mystical utterances of San Juan de la Cruz, the variegated productions of Lope de Vega, the baroque images of Góngora, and the serious and satirical poems of Quevedo. All the works of this period, including those of the national theater, showed an extraordinary diversity of form with every conceivable metrical variation.

In comparison, the eighteenth century had little poetry of the first order; it did, however, introduce a new spirit, an analysis of man's sentiments and emotional anguish close to Romanticism. This literary development, known to most European countries in the second half of the eighteenth century, may be seen in the "Epístola de Fabio a Anfriso" (Epistle from Fabio to Anfriso) by Jovellanos, a long poem in unrhymed hendecasyllables and perhaps the best of its period.

The romantic spirit of course was not new to Spain, having already been present, as many German scholars have pointed out, in the *Romancero* and the national theater of the Golden Century. It was from these two sources that many French, English, and German romantic poets drew their themes, and Spanish poets of this period in turn borrowed from their foreign contemporaries certain strophic forms, together with the freedom to combine them without forgetting their own vernacular tradition. The "Canto a Teresa" (Ode to Theresa) of Espronceda, perhaps the best Spanish love poem of this period, was written in *octavas reales*, adapted from the *ottava rima* stanza of Italian poetry.

In the nineteenth century we find two groups of poets. The

first, appearing about 1840, was close to the Romanticism of Byron. At times revolutionary, as in Espronceda, the group at other times stressed native tradition, as in the Duque de Rivas, or exotic subjects, as in Zorrilla. A second group begins about 1870 with the appearance of the two most important nineteenth-century Spanish poets, Gustavo Adolfo Bécquer and Rosalía Castro. Bécquer, a Sevillian, and Rosalía Castro, a woman from Galicia, are the true founders of modernity in Spanish poetry. In their work, form became more personal and free and there was greater emphasis on assonantal rhyme and grouping of lines of a varying number of syllables. Because of their original accent and the symbolism and mystery of their poems, they may be considered the forerunners of contemporary poetry in Spain.

The direction which that poetry was to take became apparent about 1898 with the twofold influence, both spiritual and formalistic, of Unamuno and Rubén Darío, Nicaraguan leader of the Modernista movement. From that movement came the three great poets of contemporary letters, Unamuno, Antonio Machado, and Juan Ramón Jiménez. Working independently, they raised the level of Spanish poetry to heights not reached for a long time. About 1927, when European and American literature was feeling the effects of *avant-garde* movements following World War I, Spanish poetry showed it had absorbed the vigor of these movements by presenting the work of an outstanding group of poets including García Lorca, Alberti, Salinas, and Guillén. These poets, together with those named above, have made Spanish poetry among the most brilliant in the literature of the twentieth century.

In making the selection of poems for this spoken anthology, we have had, for reasons of timing, to omit many of the longer poems one might have wished to include—the "Coplas" (Stanzas) of Jorge Manrique, the first "Égloga" (Eclogue) of Garcilaso, the seventeenth-century "Epístola moral a Fabio" (Moral Epistle to Fabio) and the above-mentioned poems by Jovellanos and Espronceda—some of them among the most important in Spanish literature. We have tried, nevertheless, to offer representative selections which would illustrate the panorama of Spanish poetry and also be interesting in themselves. Whenever possible we have chosen shorter poems, always taking into account the renown of the author and the interest and intrinsic merit of each composition.

In regard to the translations included here, we have tried simply to write a literal English version of the poems, so that the reader not familiar with Spanish may get an idea of their meaning. No attempt has been made to render a "literary" or "poetical" translation. On the contrary, in an effort not to distort meaning through any such free interpretation, we have followed as closely as possible the original text of each poem.

Eugenio Florit

New York, 1964

Cantar de Mío Cid

This epic poem, or *cantar de gesta* (*gesta*, deed), belongs to a type of poetry widely cultivated in Spain and other European countries during the first half of the twelfth century. It was composed by an unknown poet about 1140, some forty years after the Cid's death and after the composition of the *Chanson de Roland*.

The Spanish poem is distinguished by its historical character, with its author apparently interested in narrating real happenings, however much he may exaggerate to impress his audience. Thus he tells the story of Rodrigo Díaz de Vivar, known as Mío Cid ("Cid" is "lord" in Arabic), a Castilian knight who was banished from Castile after having incurred the disfavor of his sovereign, Alphonse VI. The poem's three parts, or *cantares*, relate the adventures of the Cid from the moment he leaves the city of Burgos through several years until, having won numerous battles against the Moors and taken the kingdom of Valencia, he is forgiven by his sovereign. Mío Cid died in Valencia in 1099.

Besides its intrinsic poetic interest, the poem is significant as the earliest-known major example of Spanish poetry. Written in groups of a variable number of lines, it includes 3,735 verses and employs assonantal rhyme. Interest exists on three levels: the narrative level, in which the poet relates historical facts; the dramatic level, in which dialogue reveals the psychological traits of the characters (a technique at which the author is quite successful); and the lyrical level, employing a sober, subdued lyricism appropriate for the Castilian landscape but with enough pathos to indicate the sensitivity of its warlike figures.

The poem is of further interest in revealing a different portrait of the Cid than is usually known. Other poems and ballads, or works like Corneille's later play (drawn from a play by the sixteenth-century writer Guillén de Castro), portray the warrior as a young man. The present poem, undiscovered until late in the eighteenth century, shows a more complete and credible figure—that of the mature man, husband and father, a noble and generous warrior, though ferocious enough when battling his enemies.

The human side of the Cid, together with his controlled violence, may be observed in the following excerpt from the first part of the poem, that relating to Don Rodrigo's banishment from Castile. The nine-year-old girl who speaks to him is perhaps the first female character in Spanish literature. The juxtaposition of the small girl against the shapes of warriors, arms, and horses makes for an arresting contrast.

Cantar de Mío Cid

Cantar primero
(fragmento)

El Campeador   adeliñó a su posada;
así como llegó a la puerta   fallóla bien cerrada,
por miedo del rey Alfonso,   que así lo pararan;
que si no la quebrantase   no se la abriesen por nada.

Los del mío Cid   a altas voces llaman,
los de dentro   no les querían tornar palabra.
Aguijó mío Cid,   a la puerta se llegaba,
sacó el pie de la estribera,   una ferida le daba;
no se abre la puerta   que era bien cerrada.

Una niña de nueve años   a ojo se paraba;
"Ya Campeador,   en buena ceñisteis espada!
El rey lo ha vedado,   anoche de él entró su carta,
con gran recaudo   y fuertemente sellada.
No vos osaríamos   abrir ni acoger por nada;
si no, perderíamos   los haberes y las casas
y aun además   los ojos de las caras.
Cid, en el nuestro mal   vos no ganáis nada;
mas el Criador os valga   con todas sus virtudes santas."

Esto la niña dijo   y tornóse para su casa.
Ya lo ve el Cid   que del rey no había gracia.
Partióse de la puerta,   por Burgos aguijaba,
llegó a Santa María,   luego descabalgaba;
fincó los hinojos,   de corazón rezaba.

The Cid

First Part

(excerpt)

The Campeador   went straight to his quarters;
when he came to the gate   he found it well locked.
Out of fear of King Alfonso   they had done this;
unless he break it down   they would not open for any reason.

The men of my Cid   called out in loud voices;
the men inside   were loath to reply.
My Cid spurred forward,   he came up to the gate,
he drew his foot from the stirrup,   a blow he gave the gate;
the gate did not open,   for it was well locked.

A nine-year-old girl   appeared before him.
"O Campeador,   in a happy hour you girded on your sword!
The King has forbidden it,   his order came last night,
borne with great precaution,   and firmly sealed.
We would not dare   open to you or shelter you at all,
or we would lose   our possessions and our houses,
and what is more,   the eyes in our faces.
Cid, from our misfortune   you will gain nothing;
may the Creator preserve you   with all His blessed powers."

Thus spoke the girl   and returned to her house.
Now the Cid sees   that he will get no favor from the King.
He left the gate,   spurred on to Burgos,
arrived at Santa María,   then dismounted;
he dropped to his knees   and prayed from his heart.

Diego Hurtado de Mendoza

(1364–1404)

Father of the Marqués de Santillana, Diego Hurtado de Mendoza was a distinguished member of the Castilian nobility during the reign of Henry III. He devoted much of his short life to writing, showing skill and good taste especially in his handling of light poetry. He was particularly fond of the popular vein of poems called *serranas*, or mountain songs, later admirably mastered by his son.

Of all Mendoza's poems the one most widely remembered is the *cossante* (stanza) included here. The *cossante* was a form of folk poetry widely cultivated in Galicia and Portugal during the Middle Ages and also known in Castile, and Mendoza's treatment of it reveals his keen ear and verbal grace.

A special appeal of this short piece resides in the parallel flow of its lines, with several lines repeating a single idea in slightly changed wording. The refrain at the end of each group of lines is characteristic of this type of poetry, and particularly interesting is its sensitive and unusual personification of a tree.

The text of this poem is first given in its original form; the entire poem is then repeated with modern Spanish orthography. It is this latter form that was read for the accompanying recording.

Cossante

A aquel árbol que mueve la foxa
algo se le antoxa.

Aquel árbol del bel mirar
face de maniera flores quiere dar:
algo se le antoxa.

Aquel árbol del bel veyer
face de maniera quiere florecer:
algo se le antoxa.

Face de maniera flores quiere dar:
ya se demuestra; salidlas mirar:
algo se le antoxa.

Face de maniera quiere florecer:
ya se demuestra; salidlas a ver:
algo se le antoxa.

Ya se demuestra; salidlas mirar.
Vengan las damas las fructas cortar:
algo se le antoxa.

Cossante

A aquel árbol que mueve la hoja
algo se le antoja.

Aquel árbol del bel mirar
hace de manera flores quiere dar:
álgo se le antoja.

Aquel árbol del bel veyer
hace de manera quiere florecer:
algo se le antoja.

Hace de manera flores quiere dar:
ya se demuestra; salidlas mirar:
algo se le antoja.

Hace de manera quiere florecer:
ya se demuestra; salidlas a ver:
algo se le antoja.

Ya se demuestra; salidlas mirar.
Vengan las damas las frutas cortar:
algo se le antoja.

Stanza

*That tree whose leaves are trembling
is yearning for something.*

*That tree so lovely to look at
acts as if it wants to give flowers:
it is yearning for something.*

*That tree so lovely to see
acts as if it wants to flower:
it is yearning for something.*

*It acts as if it wants to give flowers:
they are already showing; come out and look:
it is yearning for something.*

*It acts as if it wants to flower:
they are already showing; come out and see:
it is yearning for something.*

*They are already showing: come out and look.
Let the ladies come and pick the fruits:
it is yearning for something.*

Juan Ruiz, Archpriest of Hita

(1280?–1351?)

Few facts about the life of Juan Ruiz are known. The first of
Spanish humorists, he was born in Alcalá de Henares soon after
1280. In 1330, for reasons that are still uncertain, he was im-
prisoned by order of the Archbishop of Toledo, and it was during
this imprisonment that he composed his *Libro de buen amor* (Book
of Good [or Best] Love). If we do not know much about this
poet's life, we feel we know him thoroughly after reading his
verses. Few authors reveal themselves in their writings more than
Juan Ruiz does.

Apparently a man of wide culture, with a passion for life and
its pleasures, Juan Ruiz ostensibly wrote his book to guide the
human soul through the path of virtue to the love of God. In
describing human love, however, he wrote with such gusto that
one is inclined to think he preferred the life of earthly pleasures
to the more difficult path of virtue.

The *Libro de buen amor* reflects the literary currents of its times,
and corresponds in Spanish literature to the *Canterbury Tales* in
English letters. It is a mixture of serious and comic, satirical and
devotional themes written mostly in the four-line stanza called
cuaderna via, or "way of four," typical of thirteenth- and four-
teenth-century Spanish poetry and similar to the Latin Goliardic
meter used elsewhere in Europe in the twelfth century. A single
autobiographical thread joins the themes of the book: the story,
invented or true, of the Archpriest's love affairs.

The fragment we include, the satiric "Of the Qualities of Small
Women," is characteristic of Juan Ruiz's style and humor—a
dry, ironical humor at times full of color and vivaciousness.

15

Libro de buen amor

De las propiedades que las dueñas chicas han
(fragmento)

Chica es la calandria y chico el ruiseñor,
pero más dulce cantan que otra ave mayor;
la mujer que es chica, por eso es mejor;
con doñeo es más dulce que azúcar ni flor.

De la mujer pequeña no hay comparación,
terrenal paraíso es, y consolación,
solaz y alegría, placer y bendición,
mejor es en la prueba que en la salutación.

Siempre quise mujer chica más que grande ni mayor,
no es desaguisado del gran mal ser huidor;
del mal tomar lo menos, dícelo el Sabidor,
por ende, de las mujeres la mejor es la menor.

Book of Good Love

Of the Qualities of Small Women
(excerpt)

A small bird is the skylark and so is the nightingale,
yet they sing more sweetly than any larger bird;
the woman who is small is therefore the better;
when treated with affection she is sweeter than sugar or a flower.

There is nothing to be compared with a small woman,
she is an earthly paradise, and a consolation,
a solace and a joy, a pleasure and a blessing,
she is better in the testing than in the first meeting.

I always preferred a small woman to a big one,
for it is not unwise to run away from a great evil;
of evils choose the lesser, saith the Philosopher,*
therefore, with women, the smallest is the best.

* *Aristotle.*

Marqués de Santillana

(1398–1458)

Iñigo López de Mendoza (better known as the Marqués de Santillana) was a member of one of the most influential and aristocratic families in Castile. A man of wealth, he was accomplished, cultured, brave; but while we have forgotten his deeds as a knight or a warrior against John II, we remember him for several poems unequalled in Spanish literary history.

Santillana was one of the first Castilian poets to become interested in the Italian Renaissance, and he wrote a series of forty-two sonnets "made in the Italian fashion," some of them mere imitations of those of Petrarch. He wrote many other kinds of poetry—philosophical, allegorical, love poetry and courtly poetry—but perhaps best known are his ten *serranillas*, or mountain songs, written with grace and a dash of mischievousness. Like the French *pastourelles*, they tell of brief encounters between gentlemen and maidens tending cows, and of the successful—or unsuccessful—love affairs that follow.

In fifteenth-century Spain, Santillana was outstanding for his devotion to poetry and the arts. He collected what was said to have been the best library in his country, and had a wide knowledge of other European languages and literatures. He was a gentleman and a writer, and accomplished in both fields.

Serranilla

Moza tan fermosa
non vi en la frontera,
como una vaquera
de la Finojosa.

Faziendo la vía
del Calatraveño
a Sancta María,
vencido del sueño,
por tierra fragosa
perdí la carrera,
do vi la vaquera
de la Finojosa.

En un verde prado
de rosas e flores,
guardando ganado
con otros pastores,
la vi tan graciosa
que apenas creyera
que fuesse vaquera
de la Finojosa.

Non creo las rosas
de la primavera
sean tan fermosas
nin de tal manera
(fablando sin glosa),
si antes supiera
de aquella vaquera
de la Finojosa.

Non tanto mirara
su mucha beldad,
porque me dejara
en mi libertad.

Mountain Song

I never saw a girl so lovely
there by the border,
as a certain cow-girl
from La Finojosa.

As I was on my way
from Calatraveño
to Santa María,
overcome by sleep,
on a rough ground
I lost my course,
there I saw the cow-girl
from La Finojosa.

In a green meadow
full of roses and flowers,
caring for her herd
with other shepherds,
she appeared so beautiful
I could scarcely believe
that she was a cow-girl
from La Finojosa.

I do not believe
the roses of springtime
would have been of such beauty
or anything like it
(to say it plainly),
if I had known before
of that cow-girl
from La Finojosa.

I would not look too long
at her great beauty
for fear of losing
my freedom to her.

Mas dije: "Donosa
(por saber quién era),
¿dónde es la vaquera
de la Finojosa?"

Bien como riendo,
dijo: "Bien vengades;
que ya bien entiendo
lo que demandades:
non es deseosa
de amar, nin lo espera,
aquessa vaquera
de la Finojosa."

But I said: "O, graceful!"
(to find out who she was),
"Where is the cow-girl
from La Finojosa?"

In a laughing manner,
she answered: "You are welcome;
I well understand
what you ask of me:
but she is not anxious
to love, nor does she expect it,
this cow-girl
from La Finojosa."

Jorge Manrique

(1440?–1479)

Jorge Manrique was a grandnephew of Santillana and was thus related to one of the most influential and aristocratic families of the century in Castile. His father was a famous general and nobleman who after having lived a full life died in 1476.

Jorge, in the tradition of his family, wrote courtly poetry of love and was also a soldier. He was killed in 1479—only three years after his father's death—at the age of thirty-nine, while fighting on the side of Queen Isabella against La Beltraneja, an illegitimate daughter of Henry IV who was a claimant to the throne of Castile.

Manrique's accomplishment in poetry can best be seen in the long poem he wrote on his father's death—an elegy of forty-three stanzas, or *coplas*. This is not only a warm, affectionate tribute to the virtues of his father as a gentleman and a soldier, but is also a masterpiece of clarity and artistic form, a meditation on the brevity of life and on the fleeting value of worldly goods and riches. These stanzas are among the most famous and admired in the Spanish language, occupying a place comparable to François Villon's "Ballade des dames du temps jadis" in French literature.

Unfortunately, the length of Manrique's "Coplas"—so admirably translated into English by Longfellow—prevents our including it in this collection. Instead, we have chosen two short examples of Manrique's love poetry, both tender and appealing, written according to the courtly style so much in vogue in the fifteenth century. In them Manrique's directness of voice and masterly choice of words can be seen.

Dos canciones

No tardes, Muerte, que muero;
ven porque viva contigo;
quiéreme, pues que te quiero,
que con tu venida espero
no tener guerra conmigo.

Remedio de alegre vida
no le hay por ningún medio,
porque mi grave herida
es de tal parte venida
que eres tú sola remedio.

Ven aquí, pues, ya que muero;
búscame, pues que te sigo;
quiéreme, pues que te quiero,
e con tu venida espero
no tener vida conmigo.

*   *   *

Con dolorido cuidado,
desgrado, pena y dolor,
parto yo, triste amador,
de amores desamparado,
de amores, que no de amor.

Y el corazón, enemigo
de lo que mi vida quiere,
ni halla vida ni muere
ni queda ni va conmigo;
sin ventura, desdichado,
sin consuelo, sin favor,
parto yo, triste amador,
de amores desamparado,
de amores, que no de amor.

Two Songs

Do not linger, Death, for I am dying;
come, so I may live with you;
love me, because I love you,
for with your coming I hope
not to struggle with myself.

There is not, by any means,
a remedy to make life happy,
because my grave wound
has come from such a place
that only you can be my remedy.

Come, then, because I am dying;
look for me, because I follow you;
love me, because I love you,
and with your coming I hope
not to keep life in myself.

*   *   *

With a painful care,
discontent, sorrow and pain,
I depart, a sad lover,
forsaken by all my loves,
by my loves, but not by love.

And my own heart, enemy
of what my life desires,
neither finds life nor dies,
nor remains, nor goes with me;
without fortune, wretched,
without comfort, without favor,
I depart, a sad lover,
forsaken by all my loves,
by my loves, but not by love.

Ballads

A *romance*, or Spanish ballad, is a poem of popular anonymous origin presenting a variable series of eight-syllable lines with assonantal rhyme, employing as subject matter either a narrative derived from the *canciones de gesta* or an episode of a more lyrical character. Ballads began to be printed in broadsides during the fifteenth century.

The *romances* brought medieval poetry to the Golden Age and spread their themes, characters, and lyricism into the national theater. Later they influenced poets from the romantic period to the present day. Lord Byron translated them into English, other poets into many other languages; Sir Walter Scott, Goethe, Victor Hugo, Herder, Grimm, and Schlegel all praised the *romance* as the most lyrical genre in Spanish literature. Spain itself has been called the "land of the *Romancero*."

The *romances* are of many types. The *romances viejos*, or old ballads, are anonymous, orally transmitted poems which are laconic in language and fragmentary in development. They include *historical* ballads, dealing with Don Rodrigo or other heroes of Spanish medieval life; *frontier* and *Moorish* ballads, dealing with relationships between Christians and Moors; *chivalric* ballads, with subjects like Charlemagne and his Twelve Peers or King Arthur and the Knights of the Round Table; and *novelescos* and *lyrical* ballads, such as the ballad included here of Count Arnaldos. Later, after the *romances viejos*, came *artistic* ballads, written by known poets from the sixteenth century up to our own time.

The *juglar*, or popular poet, when reciting, always tried to emphasize some aspect in the life of the hero that would be of most interest to his audience. The audience in turn retained his wording, transmitting it to other audiences. In this way Spanish literature was provided with the genre most distinctly its own.

The first selection included here concerns the attempt of King John II to conquer Granada in 1431. In the ballad Granada is represented as a beautiful woman to whom the King proposes. She rejects him, saying that she is already married to her Moorish lover.

The second ballad, widely praised as one of the most interesting of its type, deals with the fictional character of Count Arnaldos, who, upon listening to the song of a sailor, asks him to teach him the song. From the approaching boat the sailor answers, in a manner that conveys the mystery of poetry, or death: "I will only tell this song to him who sails with me."

Dos romances anónimos

Abenámar

¡Abenámar, Abenámar,
moro de la morería,
el día que tú naciste
grandes señales había!
Estaba la mar en calma,
la luna estaba crecida:
moro que en tal signo nace,
no debe decir mentira!—
Allí respondiera el moro,
bien oiréis lo que decía:
—Yo te la diré, señor,
aunque me cueste la vida,
porque soy hijo de un moro
y una cristiana cautiva;
siendo yo niño y muchacho
mi madre me lo decía:
que mentira no dijese,
que era grande villanía:
por tanto pregunta, rey,
que la verdad te diría.
—Yo te agradezco, Abenámar,
aquesta tu cortesía.
¿Qué castillos son aquéllos?
¡Altos son y relucían!
—El Alhambra era, señor,
y la otra la mezquita;
los otros los Alixares,
labrados a maravilla.
El moro que los labraba
cien doblas ganaba al día,
y el día que no los labra
otras tantas se perdía.
Desque los tuvo labrados,
el rey le quitó la vida,
porque no labre otros tales
al rey del Andalucía.

Two Anonymous Ballads
Abenámar

"*Abenámar, Abenámar,*
Moor of the Moorish people,
on the day you were born
great signs appeared!
The seas were calm,
the moon was full:
a Moor born under such a sign
should never tell a lie!"
Then the Moor answered,
you shall hear what he said:
"*I will tell the truth, my lord,*
though it cost me my life,
for my father was a Moor
and my mother a captive Christian;
and when I was but a boy,
my mother used to tell me
that I should never lie,
for it is a great villainy:
so you may ask, my king,
and I will tell you the truth."
"*I thank you, Abenámar,*
for your courtesy.
What are those castles?
How high they are and how they shine!"
"*That is the Alhambra, my lord,*
and the other is the mosque;
the others, the Alixares,
fashioned so marvelously.
The Moor who worked on them
earned a hundred gold coins daily,
and the day he did not work
so many did he lose.
When his work was finished,
the king put him to death,
lest he fashion others similar
for the king of Andalusia.

El otro es Generalife,
huerta que par no tenía;
el otro Torres Bermejas,
castillo de gran valía.—
Allí habló el rey don Juan,
bien oiréis lo que decía:
—Si tú quisieses, Granada,
contigo me casaría;
daréte en arras y dote
a Córdoba y a Sevilla.
—Casada soy, rey don Juan,
casada soy, que no viuda;
el moro que a mí me tiene,
muy grande bien me quería.

The other is Generalife,
garden without equal;
the other is Torres Bermejas,
a castle of great value."
And then King John spoke,
you shall hear what he said:
"If you were willing, Granada,
I would marry you;
and for dowry I would give you
both Cordova and Seville."
"I am married, King John,
I am married, and not a widow;
and the Moor to whom I belong
loves me very well."

El conde Arnaldos

¡Quién hubiese tal ventura
sobre las aguas del mar,
como hubo el conde Arnaldos
la mañana de San Juan!
Con un falcón en la mano
la caza iba a cazar,
vió venir una galera
que a tierra quiere llegar.
Las velas traía de seda,
la ejercia de un cendal,
marinero que la manda
diciendo viene un cantar
que la mar facía en calma,
los vientos face amainar,
los peces que andan n'el hondo
arriba los face andar,
las aves que andan volando
n'el mástel las faz posar.
Allí fabló el conde Arnaldos,
bien oiréis lo que dirá:
—Por Dios te ruego, marinero,
dígasme ora ese cantar.—
Respondióle el marinero,
tal respuesta le fué a dar:
—Yo no digo esta canción
sino a quien conmigo va.

Count Arnaldos

*I'd like to have such fortune
on the waters of the sea,
as Count Arnaldos had
on the morning of St. John's Day!
With a falcon on his hand
he was going out a-hunting
when he saw a galley
approaching the shore.
Its sails were of silk,
its riggings of gauze thread,
the sailor in command
was singing a song
that calmed the sea,
made the winds subside,
made the fish at the bottom
come up to the top,
and the birds flying by
come to perch on the mast.
Then spoke Count Arnaldos,
you shall hear what he said:
"In God's name I pray you, sailor,
tell me now the song you sing."
But the sailor answered him,
and the answer was this:
"I will only tell this song
to him who sails with me."*

Garcilaso de la Vega

(1503–1536)

With Garcilaso de la Vega begins the flourishing of Renaissance poetry in Spain, and it is for this reason he may be called the starting point of the *Siglo de Oro* (Golden Century), a period extending from the middle of the sixteenth to the end of the seventeenth centuries. Garcilaso's poems were published after his death, in 1543, together with those of his close friend and fellow poet, Juan Boscán, in a book which is considered one of the most influential works in Spanish literature. By introducing Italian forms and meters into Spain the book opened the way to a flood of new poetry. It was at that time that the hendecasyllabic line became as Spanish as the eight-syllable line.

Garcilaso followed in the tradition of Santillana and Manrique in being both soldier and courtier, remarkable alike for his handsome figure, his bravery, and his culture. He served in the army of Emperor Charles V and received a wound during the campaign of Tunisia (1535). Travelling to Naples, he won the esteem and admiration of men and women alike. He was married to doña Elena de Zúñiga, but remained deeply in love with a Portuguese lady-in-waiting of the Empress, doña Isabel de Freire, to whom he refers in most of his poems. When in 1536 the Emperor freed his armies in the southeast of France, Garcilaso took part in the siege of a tower near Fréjus, where he was seriously wounded; taken to Nice, he died soon thereafter.

Garcilaso is a vivid example of the Renaissance man, skilled in music, arms, letters, as well as in the battles of love. His poetic output was not large—he left only three eclogues, five songs or odes, two elegies, one epistle, thirty-eight sonnets and some short pieces written in the traditional form of Castilian poetry—but it is of such high quality as to place him among the best poets of the European Renaissance.

The central theme of his poems is love, as shown in the two sonnets included here. Both are dedicated to doña Isabel de Freire; the second was written shortly after Garcilaso learned the news of her death. In them one finds the perfect blend of music and idea, the deep feeling for nature and love that make Garcilaso a master whose influence is ever present in Spanish poetry.

Soneto V

Escrito está en mi alma vuestro gesto,
y cuanto yo escribir de vos deseo;
vos sola lo escribistes, yo lo leo
tan solo que aun de vos me guardo en esto.

En esto estoy y estaré siempre puesto;
que aunque no cabe en mí cuanto en vos veo,
de tanto bien lo que no entiendo creo,
tomando ya la fe por presupuesto.

Yo no nací sino para quereros;
mi alma os ha cortado a su medida;
por hábito del alma misma os quiero.

Cuanto tengo confieso yo deberos;
por vos nací, por vos tengo la vida,
por vos he de morir y por vos muero.

Soneto X

¡Oh dulces prendas, por mi mal halladas,
dulces y alegres cuando Dios quería!
Juntas estáis en la memoria mía,
y con ella en mi muerte conjuradas.

¿Quién me dijera cuando en las pasadas
horas en tanto bien por vos me vía,
que me habíades de ser en algún día
con tan grave dolor representadas?

Pues en un hora junto me llevastes
todo el bien que por términos me distes,
llevadme junto el mal que me dejastes.

Si no, sospecharé que me pusistes
en tantos bienes, porque deseastes
verme morir entre memorias tristes.

Sonnet V

Your countenance is written in my soul,
and whatever I may wish to write of you;
you yourself wrote it; I read it
in such privacy that I hide even from you.

In this condition I am and always will remain;
for though I cannot contain all that I see in you,
whatever I do not comprehend of your great worth, I believe,
since my faith takes it for granted.

I was born only to love you;
my soul has cut you to its measure;
I want you as a garment for my soul.

Whatever I own I confess I owe to you;
for you I was born, for you I have life,
for you I must die and for you I am dying.

Sonnet X

Oh sweet love tokens, found to my distress,
so sweet and gay when God was willing!
You stay together in my memory
and conspire with it toward my death.

Who could have told me, who saw me in past
hours in such joy because of you,
that you would become to me one day
tokens of such deep sorrow?

Since in an hour you took away from me
all the joy you gave me only for a time,
take as well the grief you left me,

or I'll suspect that you transported me
to such a state of joy because you wished
to see me die among sad memories.

Gutierre de Cetina

(1520–1560)

The reformation which Garcilaso initiated in Castilian poetry in the first part of the sixteenth century had many followers. One of these, a minor poet but a distinguished writer of sonnets, was Gutierre de Cetina.

Cetina was born in Seville, and after an eventful life in Spain went to Italy and Germany, where he served in the army of Emperor Charles V. While in Italy he read Italian poetry, especially that of Petrarch, which he translated successfully. Afterwards he moved to Mexico, where three of his brothers and an uncle had already settled. There he continued writing poetry —sonnets, songs, elegies, and madrigals—and there he died at forty, presumably in a duel.

Cetina also wrote satirical prose, primarily a *Diálogo entre la cabeza y la gorra* (Dialogue Between the Head and the Cap). He is most famous, however, for a "Madrigal" which appears in all anthologies of Spanish poetry. It is an example of a love poem both delicate and passionate, a poem worthy of the fame it has brought its author.

Madrigal

Ojos claros, serenos,
si de un dulce mirar sois alabados,
¿por qué, si me miráis, miráis airados?
Si cuanto más piadosos,
más bellos parecéis a aquel que os mira,
no me miréis con ira,
porque no parezcáis menos hermosos.
¡Ay, tormentos rabiosos!
Ojos claros, serenos,
ya que así me miráis, miradme al menos.

Madrigal

Bright and serene eyes,
if you are praised for having a sweet glance,
why when looking at me do you look angrily?
If the kinder you are
the more beautiful you seem to him who gazes at you,
do not look at me in anger
so as not to appear less beautiful.
Oh, raging torments!
Bright and serene eyes,
even though you look at me thus, at least do look at me.

Fray Luis de León

(1527–1591)

If any city in Spain can be identified with the spirit of the Renaissance, it is the university city of Salamanca, rich in cultural tradition and the proper atmosphere for the development of arts and letters.

Fray Luis de León, born in a small town in the province of Cuenca, studied first in Madrid and Alcalá (another important university of the time) and then went to Salamanca to continue his education. Here he entered the religious order of the Augustinians, and by 1561 had become a professor at the university. In 1572, because of his criticism of the inaccuracy of the Vulgate edition of the Bible and his temerity in translating the *Song of Songs* into Spanish, Fray Luis was imprisoned in Valladolid for five years by order of the Inquisition. Upon his release, the Tribunals revoked the sentence and all his honors were restored to him. He continued teaching at the university until his death in 1591.

Fray Luis was an exceptional example of a happy combination of Christian and Renaissance elements. His was a mind apparently equally at home in the religious and secular worlds.

Other than his translations from the Latin, Greek, Hebrew, and Italian, his poetic output was small, consisting of only twenty-three poems. Many of them, however, are without equal in Spanish poetry. His odes, written in the five-line stanza called *lira* (lyre), are remarkable for the sobriety and clarity of their style, as well as for the sublimity of their ideas. Primarily of a religious theme, they reflect the contemplative spirit of their author and the intensity of his love of God. The poet's religious consciousness is shown undergoing many influences: the music of his friend Salinas, blind organist of Salamanca's cathedral (as in the ode included here); the sight of a starry night; the poet's ardent desire to view the wonders of Creation after his death.

In another vein, Fray Luis wrote an ode about the "Vida retirada" (Retired Life), one of the best renderings into Spanish of the Horatian idea of longing for a retired life in the country, as in the well-known *Beatus ille* . . . ("Blessed he, who far from business cares . . .").

The serenity and sincerity of Fray Luis' poetry has always been admired; with Garcilaso's it has been a true source of inspiration for Spanish poets of yesterday and today.

Oda a Francisco Salinas

El aire se serena
y viste de hermosura y luz no usada,
Salinas, cuando suena
la música extremada
por vuestra sabia mano gobernada.

A cuyo son divino
mi alma que en olvido está sumida,
torna a cobrar el tino
y memoria perdida
de su origen primera esclarecida.

Y como se conoce,
en suerte y pensamientos se mejora;
el oro desconoce
que el vulgo ciego adora,
la belleza caduca engañadora.

Traspasa el aire todo
hasta llegar a la más alta esfera,
y oye allí otro modo
de no perecedera
música, que es la fuente y la primera.

Ve cómo el gran maestro,
a aquesta inmensa cítara aplicado,
con movimiento diestro
produce el son sagrado
con que este eterno templo es sustentado.

Y como está compuesta
de números concordes, luego envía
consonante respuesta,
y entrambas a porfía,
se mezcla una dulcísima armonía.

Ode to Francisco Salinas

The air becomes serene
and is clothed in beauty and strange radiance,
Salinas, when there sounds
the incomparable music
governed by your skilled hands.

At that heavenly sound
my soul, that is sunk in forgetfulness,
recovers its judgment
and the lost memory
of its first, exalted origin.

And as it knows itself,
it improves its fate and thought;
it disdains the gold
that the blind multitude worships,
and perishable, deceitful beauty.

It traverses the ether
until it reaches the highest sphere,
and there it hears another mode
of imperishable
music, the first, the source of all.

It sees how the Great Master,
playing this immense cither,
with skilled movement
produces the sacred sound
by which this eternal temple is sustained.

And as it is composed
of concordant numbers, it emits
a consonant response,
and from their vying
is mingled the sweetest harmony.

Aquí la alma navega
por un mar de dulzura, y finalmente
en él ansí se anega,
que ningún accidente
extraño o peregrino oye o siente.

¡Oh desmayo dichoso!
¡oh muerte que das vida! ¡oh dulce olvido!
¡durase en tu reposo
sin ser restituido
jamás a aqueste bajo y vil sentido!

A este bien os llamo,
gloria del apolíneo sacro coro,
amigos, a quien amo
sobre todo tesoro;
que todo lo visible es triste lloro.

¡Oh!, suene de contino,
Salinas, vuestro son en mis oídos,
por quien al bien divino
despiertan los sentidos,
quedando a lo demás adormecidos.

Here the soul steers
through a sea of sweetness, and at last
sinks so deep within,
that it hears or feels
no strange or rare event.

O blessed trance!
O death that gives life! O sweet oblivion!
Could I but remain in your repose
without being restored
ever to these low and abject senses!

To this bliss I call you,
glory of Apollo's sacred choir,
friends whom I love
beyond all treasure,
since all visible things are sorrowful tears.

Oh, may your music, Salinas,
sound everlastingly in my ears;
hearing it, my senses
awaken to God's goodness,
and to all else remain oblivious.

San Juan de la Cruz

(1542–1591)

San Juan de la Cruz, whose secular name was Juan de Yepes, was born in a small town in the province of Ávila, in Castile. In 1564 he entered the religious order of the Carmelites, then went to study in the University of Salamanca. He then became a friend of Santa Teresa de Jesús (St. Theresa of Ávila), joining her in her task of reforming the Order. In accordance with Santa Teresa's ideas of sterner discipline, he founded several convents for men. When opposition to the reformation arose, San Juan was detained as a prisoner in Toledo for eight months, during which time he was said to have conceived some of his greatest poetry. After that this extraordinary man served in important positions in the Carmelite Order, in Baeza, Granada, and Ávila, and died after a brief illness in the town of Úbeda.

San Juan's literary work is a combination of prose and poetry, the former being a commentary and clarification of the mystical poems in which he tries to explain the process by which the soul, burning with divine love, finds its way through the "dark night" to its final union with God.

The poems are few in number, most of them written in the five-line *lira* stanza used by Garcilaso and Fray Luis de León. The poem included here, "Noche oscura del alma" (Dark Night of the Soul) is typical of this kind of poetry. In it, as the poet himself explains, "the soul sings the lucky venture it had in passing through the dark night of faith, in nakedness and purgation, into the union with the 'Beloved.'" Or, to explain it further, the soul, once her house is quieted down (its senses dominated), flees in a dark night on an impulse towards heaven in order to encounter her Beloved (Christ), and abandons herself in His arms.

San Juan also wrote poetry in traditional Spanish forms, such as ballads and songs with a refrain. In all his poems he is not only a master of poetical expression, delicacy, and musicality, but also the mystic who through images and metaphors succeeds in conveying the most subtle experiences of the soul in its search for, and surrender to, the Divine Lover.

Noche oscura del alma

En una noche oscura,
con ansias en amores inflamada,
¡oh dichosa ventura!
salí sin ser notada,
estando ya mi casa sosegada.

A escuras y segura,
por la secreta escala, disfrazada,
¡oh dichosa ventura!
a escuras y en celada,
estando ya mi casa sosegada.

En la noche dichosa,
en secreto, que nadie me veía,
ni yo miraba cosa,
sin otra luz y guía
sino la que en el corazón ardía.

Aquésta me guiaba,
más cierto que la luz de mediodía,
adonde me esperaba
quien yo bien me sabía,
en parte donde nadie parecía.

¡Oh noche que guiaste!
¡oh noche amable más que la alborada!
¡oh noche que juntaste
Amado con amada,
amada en el Amado transformada!

En mi pecho florido,
que entero para él sólo se guardaba,
allí quedó dormido,
y yo le regalaba,
y el ventalle de cedros aire daba.

Dark Night of the Soul

On a dark night,
burning with love's desire,
oh happy adventure!
I went out, unnoticed,
my house being already calm.

In the darkness and safe,
by the secret stair, in disguise,
oh happy adventure!
in the darkness and concealed,
my house being already calm.

On that happy night,
in secret, since no one could see me,
nor I see anything,
with no other light or guide
than that which burned in my heart.

That light guided me,
more surely than the noonday sun,
to where He was waiting
Whom I knew so well,
in a place where no one was.

Oh night that led me!
Oh night more loving than the dawn!
Oh night that brought together
the Lover and the loved,
the loved one transformed into the Lover!

On my flowering breast,
that kept itself entirely for Him alone,
He fell into deep slumber,
and I caressed Him,
cooled by the breeze from the cedars.

El aire de la almena,
cuando yo sus cabellos esparcía,
con su mano serena
en mi cuello hería,
y todos mis sentidos suspendía.

Quedéme y olvidéme,
el rostro recliné sobre el Amado;
cesó todo, y dejéme,
dejando mi cuidado
entre las azucenas olvidado.

The air from the battlement,
as I loosened His hair,
wounded my neck
with its calm hand,
and suspended all my senses.

I remained and I lost myself,
my face I rested against my Lover;
all ceased, and I was left,
leaving my cares
forgotten among the lilies.

Luis de Góngora y Argote

(1561—1627)

The most important representative of the "cultist" period in Spanish poetry was undoubtedly Luis de Góngora y Argote. Born in Cordova, in 1561, he apparently studied in Granada (he refers to his stay there in one sonnet), held a position as a priest in the Cathedral, traveled extensively in Spain, lived for some time in Madrid, where he served as a chaplain to Philip III, and died in Cordova in 1627. His life was therefore quite different from those of Lope de Vega, Cervantes, or Quevedo, his contemporaries. Góngora was a writer completely devoted to his art; and his art was, in turn, devoted to the élite. He once said, "I wish to do something: not for the many."

Góngora and "Gongorism" fill a bright but controversial page in Spanish literary history, being alternately praised or condemned according to the taste of the times. His is a poetry rich in color, accomplished in architecture, and original in its treatment of words, metaphors and imagery. Part of the general trend in seventeenth-century European poetry which appeared as Marinism in Italy, Euphuism in England, and *préciosité* in France, "Gongorism" was the Spanish form of that fashion and represents the baroque spirit in poetry.

Góngora's poetical works fall into two classes: the short poems (ballads, carols, sonnets, songs), and the long poems, those in which, as in the *Fábula de Polifemo y Galatea* (Fable of Polyphemus and Galatea) and the *Soledades* (Solitudes), the cultist manner is more pronounced.

In the first group are several charming pieces, some of them really admirable, such as the one included here, *"Romancillo"* (Little Ballad), written in traditional meter and spirit. In other instances even these short poems present a more elaborate design and a rather involved, almost rococo technique. This will be seen in the second selection, madrigal-like in mood, carefully constructed around a simple theme, that of a lover trying to gather flowers for his beloved and stung by a bee.

Romancillo

Las flores del romero,
niña Isabel,
  hoy son flores azules,
  mañana serán miel.

Celosa estás, la niña,
celosa estás de aquel
dichoso, pues lo buscas,
ciego, pues no te ve,
ingrato, pues te enoja
y confiado, pues
no se disculpa hoy
de lo que hizo ayer.
Enjuguen esperanzas
lo que lloras por él;
que celos entre aquellos
que se han querido bien,
  hoy son flores azules,
  mañana serán miel.
Aurora de ti misma,
que cuando a amanecer
a tu placer empiezas,
te eclipsa tu placer,
serénense tus ojos,
y más perlas no des,
porque al Sol le está mal
lo que a la Aurora bien.
Desata como nieblas
todo lo que no ves;
que sospechas de amantes,
y querellas después
  hoy son flores azules,
  mañana serán miel.

Little Ballad

The flowers of the rosemary,
maiden Isabel,
    today they are blue flowers,
    tomorrow they will be honey.

You are jealous, maiden,
you are jealous of one who is
lucky, because you seek him,
blind, because he does not see you,
ungrateful, because he angers you
and presumptuous, because
he does not excuse himself today
for what he did yesterday.
Let your hopes wipe away
the tears you shed for him;
for jealousies between those
who loved each other well,
    today they are blue flowers,
    tomorrow they will be honey.
Like a dawn of yourself,
when at your pleasure
you begin to brighten the day,
your own pleasure eclipses you;
let your eyes become serene,
and shed no more pearls,
for what suits the Dawn
is not becoming to the Sun.
Scatter, as if a mist,
all that you cannot see;
for suspicions in lovers,
and quarrels afterwards,
    today they are blue flowers,
    tomorrow they will be honey.

Madrigal

De la florida falda
que hoy de perlas bordó la Alba luciente,
tejidos en guirnalda
traslado estos jazmines a tu frente,
que piden, con ser flores,
blanco a tus sienes y a tu boca olores.

Guarda destos jazmines
de abejas era un escuadrón volante,
ronco sí de clarines,
mas de puntas armado de diamante;
púselas en huída,
y cada flor me cuesta una herida.

Más, Clori, que he tejido
jazmines al cabello desatado,
y más besos te pido
que abejas tuvo el escuadrón armado;
lisonjas son iguales
servir yo en flores, pagar tú en panales.

Madrigal

From the flowery slope
that gleaming Dawn embroidered today with pearls,
  wound into a garland,
these jasmines I place upon your brow,
    which, though they are flowers,
ask whiteness from your temples and perfume from your lips.

  Guardian of these jasmines
was a flying column of bees,
    though mute in clarions,
well-armed with diamond points;
    I put them to flight
and each flower cost me a wound.

  Oh Chloris, more numerous than the jasmines
I have woven into your unbound hair
      are the kisses I ask of you,
more numerous than the bees that formed the armed column;
      these are equal flatteries:
I serve you with flowers, you pay me with honeycombs.

Lope de Vega

(1562–1635)

With the exception of the picaresque novel, Lope de Vega worked in every literary genre with such spontaneity, ease, and fecundity that he was a source of amazement in his own age and remains an enigma in ours. In his day, to praise anything it was enough to say, "It is by Lope." Largely because of his part in creating Spain's national theater, he achieved an almost legendary fame. He himself admitted to writing 1800 plays, of which about 500 survive, on all subjects from the religious and mythological to the social and historical, creating, in the last category, some of his greatest achievements.

Lope's principal merit was his ability to blend—more happily than his contemporaries—traditional folklore with the spirit of Renaissance poetry, so that his plays are like crowded canvases in which one observes all forms, trends, situations, and plots of his day, all full of the sense of action that was part of his own life.

Lope was born in Madrid, where he studied before going to the University of Alcalá. He was involved in several love affairs, was married twice, and took part in the Armada as a volunteer in 1588. In 1614 he was ordained a priest, a situation that did not prevent his falling in love again. Several domestic problems, such as the death of one of his sons and the elopement of a daughter, contributed to the loss of his health, and he died in his native city at the age of seventy-three.

The turbulence of Lope's life is naturally reflected in his writings, where his excellent lyric poetry shows the same versatility, humor, sincerity, and passion that marked his actions. In the two sonnets included here (and it is interesting to note the large number of good sonnets written in Spanish), we see two of Lope's interests: human love, as shown in the collection *Rimas humanas* (Human Poems) (1602), inspired by one of his mistresses, Micaela de Luján; and religious love, as shown in his *Rimas sacras* (Sacred Poems) (1614), a volume that includes some of the best examples of this type of poetry. The second selection is particularly representative of the religious side of Lope's personality. He appears here basically human, his soul turning in repentance to the Lord, even if later he would turn again to the love of a woman. Perhaps if both sides are put together, we may see the real Lope de Vega.

Varios efectos del amor

Desmayarse, atreverse, estar furioso,
áspero, tierno, liberal, esquivo,
alentado, mortal, difunto, vivo,
leal, traidor, cobarde, animoso.

No hallar, fuera del bien, centro y reposo.
Mostrarse alegre, triste, humilde, altivo,
enojado, valiente, fugitivo,
satisfecho, ofendido, receloso.

Huir el rostro al claro desengaño,
beber veneno por licor suave,
olvidar el provecho, amar el daño.

Creer que un cielo en un infierno cabe;
dar la vida y el alma a un desengaño;
esto es amor, quien lo probó lo sabe.

Soneto XVIII

¿Qué tengo yo, que mi amistad procuras?
¿Qué interés se te sigue, Jesús mío,
que a mi puerta, cubierto de rocío,
pasas las noches del invierno oscuras?

¡Oh, cuanto fueron mis entrañas duras,
pues no te abrí! ¡Qué extraño desvarío
si de mi ingratitud el hielo frío
secó las llagas de tus plantas puras!

¡Cuántas veces el ángel me decía:
"¡Alma, asómate agora a la ventana,
verás con cuánto amor llamar porfía!"

¡Y cuántas, hermosura soberana:
"Mañana le abriremos"—respondía,
para lo mismo responder mañana!

Various Effects of Love

To be fainthearted, to be bold, to be raging mad,
surly, tender, generous, aloof,
courageous, near death, dead, alive,
loyal, treacherous, cowardly, spirited.

Not to find, beyond your lover, satisfaction or peace.
To look happy, sad, humble, arrogant,
irate, valiant, self-effacing,
satisfied, offended, distrustful.

To turn your face from clear proofs of deceit,
to drink poison as if it were a soothing liquor,
to disregard gain and delight in being injured.

To believe that heaven can lie contained in hell;
to devote your life and soul to being disillusioned;
this is love; whoever has tasted it, knows.

Sonnet XVIII

What do I have that you seek my friendship?
What do you hope to gain, oh dear Jesus,
that at my door, covered with dew,
you spend the somber nights of winter?

Oh! how cruel my heart was then,
for I did not open to you. What strange madness
if the icy chill of my ingratitude
dried out the wounds of your pure feet!

How many times the angel said to me:
"Soul, look out your window
and see how, with so much love, He persists in calling!"

And how many times, oh Supreme Beauty,
"I will open tomorrow" was my answer,
only to make the same answer the next day!

Francisco de Quevedo y Villegas

(1580–1645)

It has been said that Francisco de Quevedo y Villegas is the most complete and universal genius in Spanish literature. A politician, poet, prose writer, satirist, and diplomat, he was somehow able to express in each field the entirety of his talents. If we find anxiety and contradiction in his writings today, it is because Quevedo was more aware than his contemporaries of the state of decadence in Spain in his own time—a political and economic decadence hidden beneath the cultural extravagance of the reigns of Philip III and Philip IV.

Quevedo was born in Madrid and studied there and in Alcalá and Valladolid. Through his friendship with the influential Duke of Osuna he took part in several diplomatic affairs in Nice and Venice. With Osuna's fall from the king's favor, Quevedo suffered banishment from the court. Later he returned to Madrid and was appointed secretary to Philip IV, only to be again confined to his provincial estate in Juan Abad. In 1634 he married a distinguished lady, but they were separated within two years after their marriage.

Quevedo's poetry was not published in book form during his lifetime. Some of it shows the caricature-like vision its author had of men, a vision sometimes deformed by a sharp, cruel, violently critical nature. Typical of this nature is the first sonnet included here, the well-known "A una nariz" (To a Nose), in which the extreme use of baroque metaphor and distortion of reality produce almost a nightmare. Such characteristics can also be observed in other poems and prose pieces, as in his picaresque novel *La vida del buscón* (The Life of a Sharper) or his allegorical satire *Sueños* (Dreams). But Quevedo was primarily a serious poet, one who having been in love could write such excellent love poems as the second sonnet included here. The thought that even after death his remains will still feel love (*polvo serán, mas polvo enamorado*) makes this last line one of the most touching in Spanish poetry. He shows a mastery of concentration achieved by few other poets. Since his death no poet has been able to express so well a sense of despair, nor has any stated so eloquently the poet's role as a conscience for his native land.

A una nariz

Érase un hombre a una nariz pegado,
érase una nariz superlativa,
érase una nariz sayón y escriba,
érase un peje espada muy barbado,

era un reloj de sol mal encarado,
érase una alquitara pensativa,
érase un elefante boca arriba,
era Ovidio Nasón más narizado.

Érase un espolón de una galera,
érase una pirámide de Egito:
las doce tribus de narices era;

érase un naricísimo infinito,
muchísimo nariz, nariz tan fiera,
que en la cara de Anás fuera delito.

To a Nose

Once there was a man attached to a nose,
it was a superlative nose,
it was a nose both executioner and scribe,
it was a swordfish with a long beard,

it was a sundial badly positioned,
it was an alembic in a pensive mood,
it was an upside-down elephant,
it was Ovidius Naso, but more nasal.

It was the beak of a war galley,
it was a pyramid of Egypt:
it was the twelve tribes of noses together;

it was an infinity of nosishness,
so much nose, such a savage nose,
that on the face of Annas* it would be a crime.

* Annas (or Anás), by an etymological pun, suggests
noselessness or a-nasality.

Soneto a Lisi

Cerrar podrá mis ojos la postrera
sombra que me llevare el blanco día,
y podrá desatar esta alma mía
hora, a su afán ansioso lisonjera;

mas no de esotra parte en la ribera,
dejará la memoria en donde ardía;
nadar sabe mi llama la agua fría
y perder el respeto a ley severa.

Alma a quien todo un dios prisión ha sido,
venas que humor a tanto fuego han dado,
médulas que han gloriosamente ardido,

su cuerpo dejarán, no su cuidado;
serán ceniza, mas tendrá sentido,
polvo serán, mas polvo enamorado.

Sonnet to Lysis

The final shadow that takes from me
the brightness of daylight may close my eyes,
and may unbind my soul
with an hour that will please its anxious care;

but my soul will not leave on that other shore
the memory of where it burned;
my flame knows how to swim the cold waters,
and lose respect for stern law.

A soul for which even a god has been a prison,
veins which have fed so great a fire,
marrow which has so gloriously burned,

will abandon their body, not their cares;
will be ashes, but will keep their feeling,
dust they will be, but dust in love.

José de Espronceda

(1808–1842)

José de Espronceda is a typical product of the Romantic Age, the Spanish counterpart of Lord Byron. He belonged to a middle-class family, his father being a colonel in the army. He studied in Madrid and when still very young founded with some friends a secret political society to fight the tyranny of Ferdinand VII. After a short time in detention he went into exile, going first to Portugal, then to London, Holland, and Paris. It is believed that while in Lisbon Espronceda met a young girl, Teresa Mancha, daughter of a Spanish émigré, only to lose sight of her. Meeting her again in London, he fell in love with her. When Espronceda left England to take part in the French revolution of 1830, Teresa married a wealthy merchant; they met again in Paris, however, eloped, and went back to Madrid, where after some years of living together, Teresa abandoned her lover.

Espronceda's romance with Teresa is important because with its passion and turbulence it has been recorded in what is perhaps the best love poem of Spanish Romanticism, the "Canto a Teresa," included in the long epic *El Diablo Mundo* (The Devil World).

In 1840 Espronceda published his *Poesías líricas* (Lyrical Poems), a collection of uneven value, in which patriotic and political themes intermingle with those of an authentic lyricism. The lyricism of Espronceda's work may be seen in the excerpt given here from "A una estrella" (To a Star), in which the mystery of Creation is offset by the skepticism of a soul which did not find repose or peace in life. In the most turbulent and perhaps best of Espronceda's poems, the long narrative poem "El estudiante de Salamanca" (The Student of Salamanca), Espronceda created a new and dramatic approach to the theme of Don Juan.

In the last years of his short life Espronceda was constantly involved in politics. In 1841 he was a diplomat, and the following year he died after a brief illness, ending a life fully in accord with his romantic temperament and the troubled times in which he lived.

A una estrella
(fragmento)

¿Quién eres tú, lucero misterioso,
tímido y triste entre luceros mil,
que cuando miro tu esplendor dudoso
turbado siento el corazón latir?

¿Es acaso tu luz recuerdo triste
de otro antiguo perdido resplandor,
cuando, engañado como yo, creíste
eterna tu ventura que pasó?

Tal vez con sueños de oro la esperanza
acarició tu pura juventud,
y gloria, y paz, y amor, y venturanza,
vertió en el mundo tu primera luz.

Y al primer triunfo del amor primero,
que embalsamó en aromas el Edén,
luciste acaso, mágico lucero,
protector del misterio y del placer.

Y era tu luz voluptüosa y tierna
la que, entre flores resbalando allí,
inspiraba en el alma un ansia eterna
de amor perpetuo y de placer sin fin.

Mas, ¡ay!, que luego el bien y la alegría
en llanto y desventura se trocó:
tu esplendor empañó niebla sombría;
sólo un recuerdo al corazón quedó.

Y ahora melancólico me miras,
y tu rayo es un dardo de pesar.
Si amor aún al corazón inspiras,
es un amor sin esperanza ya.

To a Star
(excerpt)

Who are you, oh mysterious star,
so timid and sad among a thousand stars,
that when gazing at your uncertain splendor
I feel the beating of my heart disturbed?

Is your light perchance a mournful memory
of another older radiance, now lost,
when, deceived like me, you believed
eternal your now-past happiness?

Perhaps Hope, with its golden dreams,
caressed your pure youthful days,
and your first light poured into the world
glory and peace, and love, and happiness.

Perchance your light, oh magic star,
protector of mystery and of pleasure,
shone on the triumph of the primal love
that perfumed Paradise with its glory.

And it was your voluptuous and tender light
that, gliding among the flowers there,
inspired the soul with eternal longing
for everlasting love and endless joy.

Alas! soon after, happiness and joy
turned into tears and misfortune;
a somber mist covered your splendor,
and in the heart only a memory remained.

And now you gaze at me sadly,
and your beam is a dart of sorrow.
If you still inspire love in my heart,
it is a love with no more hope.

Gustavo Adolfo Bécquer

(1836–1870)

In the history of Spanish poetry Gustavo Adolfo Bécquer stands out as a writer of great sensitivity and delicacy. As a Romanticist he is both the last figure of that age and the forerunner of a new one. To the excesses of Romanticism he offered a poetry of an intimate and simple nature, a poetry of tender impressionism.

His life was short and hard. He was born in Seville, the son of a painter. When very young he became orphaned and was reared by his godmother, who gave him a good education. At the age of eighteen he went to Madrid to follow a career of letters. There he encountered only poverty and disease. After an unhappy marriage and an equally unhappy love affair he died of consumption at the age of thirty-four.

Bécquer earned his living as a journalist, producing excellent articles in carefully written prose. Shortly after his death his friends gathered his poems in a book, the *Rimas* (Rhymes). The eighty-six poems included in it constitute his only book of verse; they run the full range from first love to ultimate sadness and disillusion. In them, however, is also expressed the mystery of poetry itself, of life and death. Besides the *Rimas*, Bécquer wrote an excellent series of *Leyendas* (prose narratives) and other works.

Like Heine in German literature, Bécquer went beyond Romanticism and thus became the precursor of contemporary Spanish poetry. His poems, with their symbolist overtones and a musical quality seldom equaled, have exerted a definite influence on such modern poets as Rubén Darío and Juan Ramón Jiménez. In Bécquer the conflict between the outside world and his own dreams and fantasies is resolved in verses which are sometimes bitter, sometimes delicate, but always filled with the purest substance of poetry.

Rima I

Yo sé un himno gigante y extraño
que anuncia en la noche del alma una aurora,
y estas páginas son de ese himno
cadencias que el aire dilata en las sombras.

Yo quisiera escribirle, del hombre
domando el rebelde, mezquino idioma,
con palabras que fuesen a un tiempo
suspiros y risas, colores y notas.

Pero en vano es luchar; que no hay cifra
capaz de encerrarlo, y apenas ¡oh hermosa!
si, teniendo en mis manos las tuyas,
pudiera al oído cantártelo a solas.

Rima X

Los invisibles átomos del aire
en derredor palpitan y se inflaman;
el cielo se deshace en rayos de oro;
la tierra se estremece alborozada;
oigo flotando en olas de armonía
rumor de besos y batir de alas;
mis párpados se cierran . . . ¿Qué sucede?
—¡Es el amor que pasa!

Rhyme I

I know a giant, strange hymn
that proclaims a dawn in the night of the soul,
and these pages are cadences of that hymn,
cadences that the air spreads in the shadows.

I would like to write it, taming
man's rebellious and poor language
with words that would be at once
sighs and laughter, colors and tones.

But the struggle is in vain; there is no cipher
capable of containing it; and hardly, oh my beauty!
could I, holding your hands in mine,
softly sing it to you when we were alone.

Rhyme X

The invisible particles of the air
quiver and ignite around me;
the sky dissolves into rays of gold;
the earth shudders with joy;
I hear the murmur of kisses and the beating of wings
floating on waves of harmony;
my eyelids close . . . What can it be?
—It is love passing by!

Rima LXVI

¿De dónde vengo?.... El más horrible y áspero
    de los senderos busca:
las huellas de unos pies ensangrentados
    sobre la roca dura;
los despojos de un alma hecha jirones
    en las zarzas agudas
    te dirán el camino
    que conduce a mi cuna.

¿A dónde voy? El más sombrío y triste
    de los páramos cruza;
valle de eternas nieves y de eternas
    melancólicas brumas.
En donde esté una piedra solitaria
    sin inscripción alguna,
    donde habite el olvido,
    allí estará mi tumba.

Rhyme LXVI

Where do I come from? . . . Seek out
         the roughest, most horrible path:
the prints of feet bloodied
         on hard rock;
the tattered remnants of a soul
         laid bare by thorny bramble
         will show you the way
         that leads to my cradle.

Where am I going? . . . Pass through
         the saddest, most somber wilderness;
a valley of eternal snow and of eternal
         melancholy mists.
There where you find a solitary stone
         without any inscription,
         where oblivion dwells,
         there my tomb will be.

Rosalía Castro

(1837–1885)

Rosalía Castro is held by many critics to be on a level with Bécquer in the poetry of the nineteenth century. One of them, Azorín, considers her "one of the most delicate, most intense, most original poets Spain has ever had." For Rosalía Castro brought to Spanish literature the sad, mystery-permeated spirit of her native region, Galicia, that northwest corner of the Spanish peninsula still alive with Celtic tradition in its green mountains, gentle valleys, and rainy skies.

Rosalía (who is always referred to by her given name) was born in Santiago de Compostela and spent her childhood there and in Padron, in the manor house of her mother. Later she moved to Madrid, and in 1867 married a well-known Galician writer, Manuel Martínez Murguía. They had several children, and Rosalía led a quiet domestic life, first in Madrid, then in Padron. She died of cancer at the age of forty-eight.

Rosalía began writing in Galician, and in her native tongue she published her first two volumes, *Cantares gallegos* (Galician Songs) (1863) and *Follas novas* (New Leaves) (1884). The former volume is full of folk poetry, interpreting, as it were, the feelings of the country people in her native land; the latter is more personal and subjective, showing the influence of Bécquer and including a new and persistent note, a sense of nostalgia for the past. Rosalía then turned to the Castilian language for *En las orillas del Sar* (On the Banks of the Sar River), published shortly before her death. It is a memorable volume of poetry, full of the bitterness and disillusion that were invading the poet's soul. In some instances, as in "Las campanas" (The Bells), the tone seems near to that of Emily Dickinson, her contemporary. Like her, Rosalía before dying requested that all her unpublished manuscripts be destroyed. Rosalía's is one of the best lyric voices in modern letters.

Las campanas

Yo las amo, yo las oigo,
cual oigo el rumor del viento,
el murmurar de la fuente
o el balido del cordero.

Como los pájaros, ellas,
tan pronto asoma en los cielos
el primer rayo del alba,
le saludan con sus ecos.

Y en sus notas, que van prolongándose
por los llanos y los cerros,
hay algo de candoroso,
de apacible y de halagüeño.

Si por siempre enmudecieran,
¡qué tristeza en el aire y en el cielo!
¡qué silencio en las iglesias!
¡qué extrañeza entre los muertos!

The Bells

I love them, I hear them,
just as I hear the sound of the wind,
the babbling of the fountain
or the bleating of a lamb.

Just as the birds do, so they too,
the moment there appears in the sky
the first gleam of dawn,
greet it with their echoes.

And in their tones, that linger
over the plains and hills,
there is something candid,
peaceful and endearing.

Should they become forever mute,
what sadness in the air and sky!
what silence in the churches!
what wonder among the dead!

Miguel de Unamuno

(1864–1936)

If the university city of Salamanca of the sixteenth century may be identified with Fray Luis de León, so in our own time the names of Salamanca and Miguel de Unamuno have become inseparably linked; Unamuno taught at the university there for many years, beginning in 1891, and was its Rector for some time before his death. At other intervals he lived in Madrid, made trips through Spain and Portugal, and in 1924, after his opposition to the military dictatorship of Primo de Rivera, was banished to the Canary Islands. He subsequently resided in France and returned to Salamanca in 1931 to his position as professor and Rector.

Although Unamuno was born in Bilbao, in the Basque country, he nevertheless became so rooted in the Castilian soil as to represent the region at its best—much as did Antonio Machado, born in Seville and a Castilian by adoption.

Unamuno is also identified with the Generation of 1898, a group of writers concerned with Spain's efforts, after the loss of its last colonies in America and the Pacific, to build its future by rediscovering its own spiritual and material resources. In that struggle Unamuno became a leader, influencing Spanish life in many aspects, by his example, voice, and writings, an influence soon to be felt in other countries. His works have been translated into many languages, and he is without doubt, as Keyserling once said, "one of the most important Spaniards, from the European point of view, and probably the most important since Goya."

Unamuno has written essays, novels, plays, and poetry, and in all of these we can detect one single idea: that of man's struggle to achieve immortality, to survive mortal life by projecting himself into the future, even into eternity.

This idea, almost a *leitmotiv* for Unamuno's life, can be seen in the poem that follows. In it the poet identifies with Castile, the arid land in which he, facing the skies, feels the permanency of his country.

Unamuno's verses first appeared in 1904, when he was past forty, under the title of *Poesías*. In 1920 he published what is considered by many the best modern religious poem, "El Cristo de Velázquez" (The Christ of Velázquez), a long meditation on the famous painting by the seventeenth-century master. *Rimas de dentro* (Poems from Within) appeared three years later, followed by *Teresa* (1924), the sonnets in *De Fuerteventura a París* (From Fuerteventura to Paris) (1925), and *Romancero del destierro* (Ballads of Exile) (1928). In 1953 the Hispanic Institute of Columbia University published *Cancionero 1928–1936*, a volume containing 1,756 poems written in diary form during the last years of Unamuno's life.

Castilla

Tú me levantas, tierra de Castilla,
en la rugosa palma de tu mano,
al cielo que te enciende y te refresca,
al cielo, tu amo.

Tierra nervuda, enjuta, despejada,
madre de corazones y de brazos,
toma·el presente en ti viejos colores
del noble antaño.

Con la pradera cóncava del cielo
lindan en torno tus desnudos campos,
tiene en ti cuna el sol y en ti sepulcro
y en ti santuario.

Es todo cima tu extensión redonda
y en ti me siento al cielo levantado,
aire de cumbre es el que se respira
aquí, en tus páramos.

¡Ara gigante, tierra castellana,
a ese tu aire soltaré mis cantos,
si te son dignos bajarán al mundo
desde lo alto!

Castile

You lift me up, oh land of Castile,
in the rough palm of your hand,
to the sky that kindles you and refreshes you,
*   the sky, your master.*

Oh strong-sinewed, lean, clear land,
mother of hearts and arms,
in you the present takes on old colors
*   from the noble past.*

Your naked fields border round
the concave meadows of the sky;
the sun finds in you its cradle, its tomb
*   and its sanctuary.*

Your round extension is all summit
and in you I feel myself raised to the sky;
the air of mountain-tops is what one breathes
*   here, in your moors.*

Gigantic altar, land of Castile,
into your air I will send forth my songs;
if they are worthy of you, they will come back to earth
*   down from on high!*

Antonio Machado

(1875–1936)

Although born in Seville, Antonio Machado may be considered a Castilian poet because of his deep devotion to the Castilian landscape and character. Just as Unamuno, from the north of the peninsula, came down to live at Salamanca, so Machado, from the south, went to live first at Madrid, then at Soria, where he became a professor of French. It was here he married his wife Leonor, who died shortly after. After living for some time in Baeza in northern Andalusia, Machado moved to Segovia and Madrid, traveling to Valencia at the outbreak of the Civil War to engage in activities for the Republic. In February, 1936, heart-worn and ill, Machado traversed the Pyrenees with his mother and one brother. He died in the small French town of Colliure, by the Mediterranean, and his mother died three days later.

Machado's poetry has been characterized by Federico de Onís as being made of permanent elements, far removed from poetic fashions and literary schools. Originally under the influence of the Modernista movement at the turn of the century, Machado soon developed his personal art, a happy blending of subjectivity and simplicity, with that understanding of history and landscape which is shown in his most important book, *Campos de Castilla* (Fields of Castile). If to these themes we add another, love, we complete the diversity—and unity—of Machado's poetry. Contemporary Spanish writers have found in him a perennial source of inspiration. Perhaps no other poet since Quevedo has spoken in a voice so distinctively Spanish.

As a dramatist, Machado wrote several plays in collaboration with his brother Manuel, himself a distinguished poet. Machado's literary criticism and essays were published in an important volume in which he invented an *alter ego*, Juan de Mairena.

Machado began publishing his poetry in 1903, with *Soledades* (Solitudes), followed in 1907 by *Soledades, galerías y otros poemas* (Solitudes, Passages and Other Poems), pieces intimate and lyrical in mood. *Campos de Castilla* (1912) reflects what Gerald Brennan has described as "the passionate love for Castile which during his five years at Soria had taken possession of his whole being." Machado's later poetry tends to be epigrammatic, witty, and of a more intellectual nature, without losing its characteristic quality. His *Obras completas* (Complete Works) have been published in many editions, beginning with that of 1917.

Yo voy soñando caminos

Yo voy soñando caminos
de la tarde. ¡Las colinas
doradas, los verdes pinos,
las polvorientas encinas!...
¿Adónde el camino irá?
Yo voy cantando, viajero
a lo largo del sendero...
—La tarde cayendo está—.
"En el corazón tenía
la espina de una pasión;
logré arrancármela un día,
ya no siento el corazón."

Y todo el campo un momento
se queda mudo y sombrío,
meditando. Suena el viento
en los álamos del río.

La tarde más se oscurece,
y el camino que serpea
y débilmente blanquea
se enturbia y desaparece.

Mi cantar vuelve a plañir:
"Aguda espina dorada,
quién te pudiera sentir
en el corazón clavada."

I Go Along Dreaming Roads

I go along dreaming roads
of the twilight. Golden hills,
green pines,
dust-laden oaks! . . .
Where can this road lead?
I go along singing, a traveler
along the trail . . .
—Night is falling now—.
"Once I had in my heart
the thorn of a passion;
one day I finally drew it out,
now I no longer feel my heart."

And all the countryside for a moment
remains silent and somber,
meditating. The wind sounds
in the poplars along the river.

The twilight deepens,
and the road that winds
and feebly fades
darkens and disappears.

Again my song tolls out:
"Oh sharp golden thorn,
could I but feel you once more
driven into my heart."

Juan Ramón Jiménez

(1881–1958)

The place of Juan Ramón Jiménez in contemporary Spanish poetry as a master and an example of absolute dedication was recognized in 1956 when he was awarded the Nobel Prize for literature. No other writer of his generation has done more to renew the use of metaphor, the play of words, and magical combinations of sounds in his country's poetry.

An Andalusian from the small town of Moguer, near the ocean, Jiménez moved to Madrid in 1900, where he lived for many years, except for a brief trip to New York in 1916 to marry his Spanish fiancée. When the Civil War interrupted this phase of his life, he returned to America with his devoted wife Zenobia and lived during 1936 and 1937 in Puerto Rico and Cuba. Later he and his wife lived in New York, Washington, D.C., and Coral Gables, only to return to Puerto Rico, where his wife died in 1956. After a long period of depression and melancholy, from which he had suffered since his youth, Jiménez died in Puerto Rico in 1958.

The rich output of Jiménez's writings can hardly be evaluated here. His is a poetry which has, since its first appearance in 1900, shown a very definite style, developing over the years into a deeper and more transcendental concept of lyric or philosophical ideas. *Arias tristes* (Sad Songs) (1903), Jiménez's first important volume, showed a blend of traditional and modern trends. The publication in 1917, however, of his *Diario de un poeta reciencasado* (Diary of a Newly Wed Poet) marked a turning point in his work and in Spanish poetry at large, a turning toward a freer verse with a more daring use of images and metaphors than before. Jiménez's final work, written in America after 1936, is remarkable for the depth of his feeling, his almost philosophical approach to poetry, and a sense of nostalgia for his native land.

The poem included here, "Primavera amarilla" (Yellow Spring), belongs to an early period, that of the volume entitled *Poemas májicos y dolientes* (Magic and Doleful Poems) (1909). It is a moving short piece full of the charm of nature, which to Jiménez was a constant source of inspiration, the colors and shapes of which were to be translated into all possible combinations in his poems and his prose.

Jiménez's best-known book of prose, *Platero y yo* (Platero and I), has been translated into many languages. It is considered to be the most beautiful work of poetic prose in Spanish.

Primavera amarilla

Abril venía, lleno
todo de flores amarillas:
amarillo el arroyo,
amarillo el vallado, la colina,
el cementerio de los niños,
el huerto aquel donde el amor vivía.

El sol unjía de amarillo el mundo,
con sus luces caídas;
¡ay, por los lirios áureos,
el agua de oro, tibia;
las amarillas mariposas
sobre las rosas amarillas!

Guirnaldas amarillas escalaban
los árboles; el día
era una gracia perfumada de oro,
en un dorado despertar de vida.
Entre los huesos de los muertos,
abría Dios sus manos amarillas.

Yellow Spring

April was coming, full
of yellow flowers:
the brook was yellow,
the fence, the hill were yellow,
the children's cemetery,
that orchard where love used to live.

The sun anointed the world in yellow
with its fallen light;
ah, among the golden lilies,
the warm, the golden water;
the yellow butterflies
over yellow roses!

Yellow garlands were climbing
the trees; the day
was a gold-incensed blessing,
in a golden awakening of life.
Among the bones of the dead,
God opened His yellow hands.

León Felipe

(1884–1968)

León Felipe Camino belongs to that group of writers constituting a link between the Generation of 1898 and contemporary writers. He began his career as a poet about 1920, when he was thirty-six, under the influence of Unamuno and Antonio Machado, but he soon turned to a kind of poetry that was moral in mood and concerned with the destiny of man and the evils of contemporary society.

León Felipe, along with many of his brother artists, left Spain because of the Civil War of 1936–1939. Unlike most of his fellow writers, however, he was a man of a restless nature, in constant struggle with conventions, whether political or literary. He was an actor, pharmacist, professor, political agitator, and lecturer. In this respect he said: "Everything there is in the world is mine and worth being part of a poem, to feed the bonfire; *everything*, even what is *literary* as long as it is ardent and is consumed by fire."

León Felipe's poetry is generally emphatic, recalling Whitman's, which he has successfully translated. His voice is almost always distinct and direct, and although he speaks in Biblical tones in much of his work—in books like *El poeta prometeico* (The Promethean Poet) and *El poeta maldito* (The Damned Poet)—he also manages to be humble and simple, as in the tone of his first volume, *Versos y oraciones de caminante* (Poems and Prayers of a Wanderer) (1920). As Whitman sings of himself in long lines but identifies also with quiet things, so León Felipe, who writes in a prophetic vein, speaks of himself in the poem included here as being like a little stone.

Como tú ...

Así es mi vida,
piedra,
como tú. Como tú,
piedra pequeña;
como tú,
piedra ligera;
como tú,
canto que ruedas
por las calzadas
y por las veredas;
como tú,
guijarro humilde de las carreteras;
como tú,
que en días de tormenta
te hundes
en el cielo de la tierra
y luego
centelleas
bajo los cascos
y bajo las ruedas;
como tú, que no has servido
para ser ni piedra
de una lonja,
ni piedra de una audiencia,
ni piedra de un palacio,
ni piedra de una iglesia;
como tú,
piedra aventurera;
como tú,
que tal vez estás hecha
sólo para ser una honda,
piedra pequeña
y
ligera ...

Like You

That's what my life is like,
stone,
like you. Like you,
small stone;
like you,
light stone;
like you,
pebble rolling
down highways
and footpaths;
like you,
the humble cobblestone in the highroads;
like you,
who in stormy days
bury yourself
in the sky of the earth
and then
glint
under the horses' hoofs
and under the wheels;
like you, not good enough to be used
either as a stone
in a market place,
or a stone in a courthouse,
or a stone in a palace,
or a stone in a church;
like you,
wandering stone;
like you,
perhaps made only
to be a slingstone,
you, small
and
light stone . . .

Pedro Salinas

(1892–1951)

Among the group of poets we call the Generation of 1927—
because in that year many published their first or most important
volumes of verse and because it was in that year that the "young

literature" came to be recognized as a serious contribution to Spanish letters—four writers may be considered representative. Two were Andalusian—García Lorca and Alberti—close to popular inspiration and reflecting in their work the color and warmth of their landscape and atmosphere. The other two, Salinas and Guillén, born in Madrid and Valladolid respectively, were scholars, close to the light and simplicity of the Castilian landscape and writing a poetry less sensuous and of a more intellectual quality than either of the two Andalusian poets.

Pedro Salinas taught in Seville, Murcia, Paris, Cambridge, and Madrid before coming to America. In Puerto Rico, Massachusetts (Wellesley), Maryland (Johns Hopkins), and Vermont (Middlebury), he established himself as a witty and brilliant teacher who in addition to writing poetry also wrote excellent literary criticism.

Salinas's poetry was first published in Madrid in 1923 in a book entitled *Seguro azar* (Sure Hazard), after which several others appeared, including *La voz a ti debida* (The Voice Owed to You) (1934) and *Razón de amor* (Reason for Love) (1936). In America he wrote *El Contemplado* (translated into English as *Sea of San Juan*) and two other books.

Salinas's poetry is fundamentally a poetry of love, centered about a feminine figure. This figure appears to be close to the author in a modern world of telephones, clocks, bars, and beaches but at the same time transcends those things so that they are converted into intellectualized, unsentimental concepts. Salinas transforms his surroundings—realistic or existential—into poetry by injecting them with the strength of a lyrical temperament always fresh and happy to be alive and in love. Even in an apparently sad poem like "Muertes" (Deaths)—the subject of which is oblivion rather than death—the subject matter is dealt with in a "civilized" mood, without any trace of sentimentality but with deep feeling.

In his last years, the growing problems of contemporary civilization drove Salinas to the writing of "Zero," a poem concerned with the destruction of the world by the atomic bomb. It is an extraordinary poem, full of the sense of tragedy and anxiety so much a part of our contemporary world.

Muertes

Primero te olvidé en tu voz.
Si ahora hablases aquí,
a mi lado,
preguntaría yo: "¿Quién es?"

Luego se me olvidó de ti tu paso.
Si una sombra se esquiva
entre el viento, de carne,
ya no sé si eres tú.

Te deshojaste toda lentamente,
delante de un invierno: la sonrisa,
la mirada, el color del traje, el número
de los zapatos.

Te deshojaste aún más:
se te cayó tu carne, tu cuerpo.
Y me quedó tu nombre, siete letras, de ti.
Y tú, viviendo,
desesperadamente agonizante,
en ellas, con alma y cuerpo.
Tu esqueleto, sus trazos,
tu voz, tu risa, siete letras, ellas.
Y decirlas tu solo cuerpo ya.

Se me olvidó tu nombre.
Las siete letras andan desatadas;
no se conocen.
Pasan anuncios en tranvías; letras
se encienden en colores a la noche,
van en sobres diciendo
otros nombres.
Por allí andarás tú,
disuelta ya, deshecha e imposible.
Andarás tú, tu nombre, que eras tú,
ascendido
hasta unos cielos tontos,
en una gloria abstracta de alfabeto.

Deaths

First I forgot you in your voice.
If you were to speak here now,
next to me,
I'd ask: "Who is it?"

Then it was your walk I forgot.
If a shadow of flesh withdraws
into the wind,
I no longer know if it's you.

You dropped your leaves slowly,
before a winter: your smile,
your look, the color of your dress, the size
of your shoes.

You dropped more leaves:
your flesh fell away from you, your body.
And only your name remained with me, seven letters of you.
And you still living in them,
desperately agonizing,
with body and soul.
Your skeleton, their tracery,
your voice, your laughter, seven letters, them.
Now your body was only the pronouncing of them.

I forgot your name.
Those seven letters go by unrelated;
they do not know each other.
Streetcar advertisements pass by; letters
flare up in colors at night;
they go on envelopes, spelling
other people's names.
And you may be there,
dissolved, destroyed and incredible.
You may be there, your name, which was you,
gone up
into some silly skies,
in an abstract glory of alphabet.

Jorge Guillén

(1893–1984)

Jorge Guillén was born in Valladolid, in Castile. He lived a life very much like that of his lifelong friend Salinas. Both married when young, had two children, and led happily married lives; Guillén was also a teacher, and taught in Paris, Murcia, Seville, Oxford, Middlebury and Wellesley College, where he gave classes from 1938 until his retirement in 1960.

Guillén's first volume of poetry was *Cántico* (Canticle), published in 1928 and considerably enlarged in three more editions, the last being that of Buenos Aires in 1950. At that time he started another series of poems under the general title of *Clamor*.

It has been said that Guillén's poetry is the most classical in contemporary Spanish poetry, though we must not take that phrase to mean a return to the themes or moods of the classic period. Guillén's poetry is "classic" in the sense that it is permanent and not subject to the fashions of an epoch. He frequently uses short meters and provides a poetic interpretation of things he sees and admires. His poetry is for the most part full of wonder and joy, as if the poet were being born each day to the marvels of the world, although his later books are more concerned with political and ideological questions.

In contrast with that of Salinas, Guillén's is not a poetry of love, and for that reason may be less appealing to the general public. Its "purity," its intellectual quality, makes it more difficult to understand. On the other hand, it is so admirably balanced and its wording so appropriate that few contemporary poets can compare with Guillén in achievement.

A good example of all these qualities may be seen in the poem included here, "Los Nombres" (Names). In it we can detect Guillén's taste for the precise and the exact. Things come alive by the mastery with which the poet treats them in the poem. An economy of words is also characteristic of Guillén's poetry, especially in the *Cántico*, to which collection this poem belongs.

Los nombres

Albor. El horizonte
entreabre sus pestañas
y empieza a ver. ¿Qué? Nombres.
Están sobre la pátina

de las cosas. La rosa
se llama todavía
hoy rosa, y la memoria
de su tránsito, prisa,

prisa de vivir más.
¡A largo amor nos alce
esa pujanza agraz
del Instante, tan ágil

que en llegando a su meta
corre a imponer   Después!
¡Alerta, alerta, alerta!
yo seré, yo seré!

¿Y las rosas? Pestañas
cerradas: horizonte
final. ¿Acaso nada?
Pero quedan los nombres.

Names

Daybreak. The horizon
half opens its lashes
and begins to see. What? Names.
They are over the patina

of things. The rose
today is still called a rose,
and the memory
of its passing, haste,

a haste to live longer.
May we be lifted to an enduring love
by this unripe power
of the Moment, so nimble

that on reaching its goal
it runs to impose   Afterwards!
On guard! On guard! On guard!
I will be! I will be!

But the roses? Fast-closed
lashes: ultimate
horizon. Perhaps nothing?
But the names remain.

Federico García Lorca

(1898–1936)

Federico García Lorca is perhaps the most widely known Spanish poet and dramatist in contemporary literature, his plays being produced in many countries and his poetry being translated and commented upon in every corner of the world.

García Lorca was born in the province of Granada, where he studied philosophy and law. After 1919 he resided primarily in Madrid, traveling in 1929–1930 to New York and Cuba, and later to Buenos Aires, where his plays were produced with great success. He was in Granada at the time the Civil War broke out, and it was there he met his tragic death at the hands of the Falangists, one of the most stupid crimes of that war. It ended the life of a true literary genius as extraordinary as Spain has ever known.

Like Lope de Vega, with whom he has frequently been compared, García Lorca had a special gusto for folk poetry, as shown in his first important volumes, *Canciones* (Songs) (1927) and *Romancero gitano.* (Gypsy Ballads) (1928). These two books established Lorca as a poet of the first rank. *Romancero gitano*, with its artistic treatment of Andalusian subjects, filled with dramatic tension and a sense of mystery no other collection of ballads had had for centuries, was one of the best collections ever published in Spain. Traditional in treatment, García Lorca's poems show a modern use of metaphor and a poetical language of great originality and beauty.

The tension and mystery of García Lorca's work are evident in the poem included here. The ballad "Romance de la luna, luna" (Ballad of the Moon, Moon) dramatizes the old superstition of the malevolent influence of moonlight, which in this case provokes the death of a child left alone in the forge while his family is away.

García Lorca's gifts for dramatization are best exemplified in his plays. In them, too, folklore, poetry, mystery, and tradition are blended for maximum effect. On the other hand, a rather surrealistic treatment of life and persons—the reality of the city—is shown in his volume of poems, *Poeta en Nueva York* (Poet in New York), which is closely related to the *avant-garde* poetry of the 1930's in its view of the human soul in the drama of contemporary civilization.

Romance de la luna, luna

La luna vino a la fragua
con su polisón de nardos.
El niño la mira mira.
El niño la está mirando.
En el aire conmovido
mueve la luna sus brazos
y enseña, lúbrica y pura,
sus senos de duro estaño.
Huye luna, luna, luna.
Si vinieran los gitanos,
harían con tu corazón
collares y anillos blancos.
Niño, déjame que baile.
Cuando vengan los gitanos
te encontrarán sobre el yunque
con los ojillos cerrados.
Huye luna, luna, luna,
que ya siento sus caballos.
Niño, déjame, no pises
mi blancor almidonado.

El jinete se acercaba
tocando el tambor del llano.
Dentro de la fragua, el niño
tiene los ojos cerrados.

Por el olivar venían,
bronce y sueño, los gitanos.
Las cabezas levantadas
y los ojos entornados.

Cómo canta la zumaya,
¡ay, cómo canta en el árbol!
Por el cielo va la luna
con un niño de la mano.

Ballad of the Moon, Moon

The moon came to the forge
in her bustle of spikenard.
The child looks and looks.
The child is looking at her.
In the sympathetic air
the moon waves her arms
and discloses, lewd and chaste,
her breasts of hard tin.
Run away, moon, moon, moon!
If the gypsies should come,
they would make from your heart
white necklaces and white rings.
Child, let me go on dancing.
When the gypsies come
they will find you on the anvil
with your little eyes closed.
Run away, moon, moon, moon!
for already I hear their horses.
Child, let me alone, do not step
on my starched whiteness.

The horseman was approaching,
beating the drum of the plain.
Inside the forge,
the child's eyes are closed.

Through the olive grove came,
bronze and dream, the gypsies.
Their heads lifted upright
and their eyes half closed.

Oh, how the owl is hooting,
oh, how it hoots in the tree!
The moon goes through the sky
with a child by the hand.

Dentro de la fragua lloran,
dando gritos, los gitanos.
El aire la vela, vela.
El aire la está velando.

The gypsies inside the forge,
are weeping, crying loudly.
The air watches and watches.
The air is watching it.

Dámaso Alonso

(1898–1990)

Dámaso Alonso was born in Madrid. A professor of philology at the University of Madrid, he was a member of an important group of writers who were poets and essayists as well as dedicated teachers.

Alonso was also a distinguished poet in his own right, whose first book, *Poemas puros: Poemillas de la ciudad* (Pure Poems: Little Poems of the City), appeared in 1921 at the beginning of the renaissance in contemporary poetry. "Los Contadores de Estrellas" (The Star Counters), included here, is from that volume. Simple and direct, it shows the relationship of its author with some of the *avant-garde* trends of those years. Alonso also published two more volumes of verse, both appearing in 1944—*Oscura noticia* (Dark News) and *Hijos de la ira* (Children of Wrath). The latter is his most personal work. His is a poetry of religious inspiration, but so strong in its tone and of such bitterness and dramatic impact that it reminds us somewhat of Unamuno's, though its pathos seems even stronger in reflecting the restlessness and anguish of contemporary man.

Dámaso Alonso and Vicente Aleixandre, each working independently, had a great influence on younger poets. Their mastery and the sincerity of their voices were highly respected. In the years after the Civil War Aleixandre and Alonso were able to help fill the vacuum in which younger writers found themselves before they could once more get in touch with the world outside Spain.

Los contadores de estrellas

Yo estoy cansado.
                        Miro
esta ciudad
                —una ciudad cualquiera—
donde ha veinte años vivo.

Todo está igual.
                        Un niño
inútilmente cuenta las estrellas
en el balcón vecino.

Yo me pongo también . . .
Pero él va más de prisa: no consigo
alcanzarle:
                Una, dos, tres, cuatro,
cinco . . .

No consigo
alcanzarle: Una, . . . dos . .
tres . . .
                cuatro . . .
                        cinco . . .

The Star Counters

I am tired.
            I contemplate
this town
            —a town like any other—
where I have lived for twenty years.

Nothing has changed.
                    A child
is uselessly counting the stars
on the next balcony.

I also try . . .
But he is faster: I cannot
catch up with him:
                    One, two, three, four,
five . . .

I cannot
catch up with him: One, . . . two . . .
three . . .
        four . . .
                five . . .

Emilio Prados

(1899–1962)

Like Aleixandre and others of his generation, Emilio Prados was an Andalusian, born in Málaga. He was a solitary child, prone to meditation, and a lover of nature, unhappy in the city or among social conventions. In 1915 he went to Madrid to continue his studies in history, the classics, and modern poets. He traveled in Europe, primarily in Germany, before returning to his home town, where he published the literary magazine *Litoral*. It was through this editorial enterprise that many important books of poetry were published, by such writers as Alberti, Cernuda, and Aleixandre.

During the Republic, Prados took an active part in politics, writing ballads to encourage the defense of the Spanish people against Fascism. In 1936 he left Spain for Paris and for Mexico, where he lived until his death, leading a solitary life while remaining in friendly contact with the world about him.

Prados's poetical career began in 1920 and continued until his death, remaining constant in its contemplation of nature and man's place in it. It could be said of Prados that he was a .poet of constant wonder. Another feature of Prados's poetry is its close relationship with traditional forms such as the ballad and short song; it is this relationship that gives his work its distinctive flavor, the charm always to be found in Spanish poetry.

Jardín cerrado (Enclosed Garden) (1946), a book rich in meaning and diverse in forms, is considered the masterpiece of this poet who continued to grow closer to an "objective contemplation of what is eternal." The poem included here, a short meditation of a man's dream about the sea as recreated in his memory, belongs to this book.

Página fiel

Nostalgia

Lejano mar, ¿conoces tu misterio?...
Sobre tu playa, el sueño
diminuto de un hombre
no se queda olvidado,
como en el alma el pensamiento,
—pétalo, sol y nácar—,
en la espalda del tiempo...

... Lejano mar:
sobre tu arena está mi cuerpo,
sobre la sombra de su cuerpo,
y sueña, sueña, sueña en ti dormido,
que sin ti vive como estoy despierto,
con la frente en el agua y los ojos sedientos,
viviendo el mar, mi sangre, en tu recuerdo.

Faithful Page

Nostalgia

Distant sea, do you know your mystery? . . .
There, upon your shore,
the smallest dream of man
does not remain forgotten,
as in the soul the thought
—petal, sun and mother-of-pearl—,
on the shoulders of time . . .

. . . Distant sea:
my body lies upon your sand,
over the shadow of its body,
and it dreams, dreams, dreams, asleep within you,
that it lives without you like me when I am awake,
with my forehead in the water and my eyes full of thirst,
while the sea lives, my blood, in your memory.

Vicente Aleixandre

(1900–1984)

An Andalusian like so many other Spanish poets, Vicente Aleixandre was born in Seville. Like many others, he moved to Madrid, where because of delicate health he lived a rather secluded life devoted primarily to writing.

Aleixandre's first volume was *Ámbito* (Space) (1928). He belonged to the group known as the Generation of 1927, a group linked by friendship and common ideals until the outbreak of the Civil War. When some members of the group went into exile, others remained in Spain, particularly Aleixandre and Dámaso Alonso, who were for years the mentors and senior poets of the younger generation and formed a bridge between them and the 1927 group.

Aleixandre's poetry is a happy mixture of Romantic spirit and surrealistic expression, a poetry of ideas written in free verse. In it we find a deep concern for man, for human reality in its connection with nature, which forms a general background to his work. *Sombra del Paraíso* (Shadow of Paradise) appeared after a long silence in 1944 and established its author as one of the leading Spanish poets of this century. From that time on he wrote continuously, one of his later books being *En un vasto dominio* (In a vast realm) (1962). "El Visitante" (The Visitor), included here, taken from a previous book, *Historia del corazón* (History of the Heart) (1954), is an excellent example of Aleixandre's blending of reality and mystery.

El visitante

Aquí también entré, en esta casa.
Aquí vi a la madre cómo cosía.
Una niña, casi mujer (alguien diría: qué alta, qué guapa se está
     poniendo),
alzó sus grandes ojos oscuros, que no me miraban.
Otro chiquillo, una menuda sombra, apenas un grito, un ruidillo
     por el suelo,
tocó mis piernas suavemente, sin verme.
Fuera, a la entrada, un hombre golpeaba, confiado, en un hierro.

Y entré, y no me vieron.
Entré por una puerta, para salir por otra.
Un viento pareció mover aquellos vestidos.
Y la hija alzó su cara, sus grandes ojos vagos y llevó a su frente
     sus dedos.
Un suspiro profundo y silencioso exhaló el pecho de la madre.
El niño se sintió cansado y dulcemente cerró los ojos.
El padre detuvo su maza y dejó su mirada en la raya azul del
     crepúsculo.

The Visitor

Here too I entered, in this house.
Here I saw the mother sewing.
A girl, almost a woman (one would say: how tall, how beautiful she is
    becoming),
raised her large dark eyes, that were not looking at me.
Another child, a tiny shadow, hardly a cry, a small noise on the floor,
touched my legs gently, without noticing me.
Outside, near the door, an unworried man was hammering on a piece of
    iron.

I entered, but nobody noticed me.
I entered through one door to go out through another.
A wind seemed to shake their clothes.
And the girl raised her face, her big, vague eyes, and raised her fingers to
    her forehead.
A deep, quiet sigh escaped the mother's breast.
The child felt tired and softly closed his eyes.
The father stayed his hammer and set his gaze on the blue line of the
    twilight.

Rafael Alberti

(b. 1903)

Born in the southwest of Spain in the province of Cádiz, Rafael Alberti pursued his first studies there and in 1917 moved to Madrid, where he engaged in painting, a form of art in which he is greatly gifted. One of his most interesting books is the long poem *A la pintura* (To Painting) (1950).

In Madrid Alberti first devoted himself to writing. He published several volumes of poetry, the first of which, *Marinero en tierra* (A Sailor Ashore) was awarded the National Prize for Literature in 1924. Still another book, *Sobre los ángeles* (About Angels) (1929), was close in imagery and atmosphere to surrealism. Considered Alberti's masterpiece, it is of undeniable importance in contemporary Spanish poetry.

Alberti belongs to a period of intense activity in Spanish literature, when such friends and fellow members of the Generation of 1927 as García Lorca, Salinas, Guillén, Cernuda, and Alonso were injecting a new youthful spirit into Spanish literature and helping to place it on a level with that of the rest of Europe. Like many of the others, Alberti combined a literary career with political activities. He became a member of the Communist Party; when the Civil War ended he went into exile, and after 1939 he lived in Argentina. He has traveled in Europe and Spanish America, and has published several volumes in which can be seen his unending love for his mother country and for his native city, together with his lifelong devotion to painting.

Alberti's writings can be grouped into various creative periods, corresponding to different epochs in his life. There is the first period of youthful grace, connected with the Spanish folk tradition (as in *Marinero en tierra*). There is a second period in which the poet shows his concern with serious problems of his restless soul (*Sobre los ángeles*). Then appear the political poems, belonging to the period of the Civil War and the first years of his exile. Later, without at all abandoning his political credo, Alberti returns to a poetry of simplicity and emotion, akin to that of his first poems. And in such books as *Retornos de lo vivo lejano* (Returns of the Distant Life) and *Ora marítima* (for which Alberti used the title of the Roman poet Rufius Festus Avienus's description of the coasts of the Mediterranean), both published in Buenos Aires in 1953, he achieves a truly felt lyricism using the simplest of stanzas.

El ángel bueno

Vino el que yo quería,
el que yo llamaba.

No aquel que barre cielos sin defensas,
luceros sin cabañas,
lunas sin patria,
nieves.
Nieves de esas caídas de una mano,
un nombre,
un sueño,
una frente.

No aquel que a sus cabellos
ató la muerte.

El que yo quería.

Sin arañar los aires,
sin herir hojas ni mover cristales.

Aquel que a sus cabellos
ató el silencio.

Para sin lastimarme,
cavar una ribera de luz dulce en mi pecho
y hacerme el alma navegable.

The Good Angel

The one that I wanted came,
the one I called.

Not the sweeper of defenseless skies,
stars without huts,
moons without a country,
snows.
Those snows that fell from a hand,
a name,
a dream,
a brow.

Not the one that tied death
to his hair.

The one that I wanted.

Without scratching the air,
or wounding leaves or shaking windows.

The one that tied silence
to his hair.

So as, without hurting me,
to dig a bank of soft light in my breast
and make my soul navigable.

Luis Cernuda

(1904—1963)

One of the more gifted of the group of poets born at the turn of the century, Luis Cernuda became officially part of the Generation of 1927 by publishing that year his first volume of poetry, *Perfil del aire* (Profile of the Air), a book highly praised for the transparency of its poems and an angel-like gift of grace. After spending his early years in his native Seville and living for some time in Madrid, Cernuda left Spain because of the Civil War. He lectured in England, the United States, and Mexico, where he lived for several years. He also made excellent translations of English poetry.

In 1936 Cernuda published his second volume, *La realidad y el deseo* (Reality and Desire), followed by several more volumes of poetry and prose essays and criticism.

Cernuda's poetry is very personal, romantic in mood although well rooted in the Spanish classical tradition. Aloof and of a rather timid nature, Cernuda shows his obsession with solitude in his sad, restrained, and sometimes bitter poetry. A pessimistic tone, disdainful of the world about him, pervades his poems.

This mood is exemplified in the poem included here. Its title is taken from a line of Bécquer (*see* p. 80 above), and its mood is quite close to the spirit of the Romantic; added to its Romanticism, however, is a purely modern feeling of desolation and anguish, so that the poem illustrates, as does all of Cernuda's work, a personal struggle between the real and the ideal.

Donde habite el olvido

Donde habite el olvido,
en los vastos jardines sin aurora;
donde yo sólo sea
memoria de una piedra sepultada entre ortigas
sobre la cual el viento escapa a sus insomnios.

Donde mi nombre deje
al cuerpo que designa en brazos de los siglos,
donde el deseo no exista.

En esa gran región donde el amor, ángel terrible,
no esconda como acero
en mi pecho su ala,
sonriendo lleno de gracia aérea mientras crece el
        tormento.

Allá donde termine este afán que exige un dueño a
        imagen suya,
sometiendo a otra vida su vida,
sin más horizonte que otros ojos frente a frente.

Donde penas y dichas no sean más que nombres,
cielo y tierra nativos en torno de un recuerdo;
donde al fin quede libre sin saberlo yo mismo,
disuelto en niebla, ausencia,
ausencia leve como carne de niño.

Allá, allá lejos;
donde habite el olvido.

Where Oblivion Dwells

Where oblivion dwells,
in the vast gardens without daybreak;
where I will be only
the memory of a stone buried among nettles
over which the wind flees from its sleeplessness.

Where my name will leave
the body it identifies in the arms of time,
where desire does not exist.

In that vast region where love, that terrible angel,
will not bury its wings
like steel in my heart,
smiling, full of airy grace, while the torment increases.

There, where will end this anxiety that demands
a master in its own image,
surrendering its life to another life,
with no further horizon than other eyes face to face.

Where sorrow and happiness will be only names,
native sky and earth around a memory;
where at last I will be free, without noticing it,
vanished into mist, into absence,
an absence as soft as a child's skin.

There, far away;
where oblivion dwells.

Miguel Hernández

(1910–1942)

The death of Miguel Hernández from consumption and lack of proper care in a prison where he had been confined since the end of the Spanish Civil War deprived Spain of an excellent poet who, had he been treated differently, might have gone on to write his most personal verse. He was a shepherd for some time when he was young, having gone for but a short time to school; thereafter he can be said to have been a self-educated man. He read poetry with dedication and soon began to write it in his native town of Orihuela and then in Madrid. Having made a first trip to the capital in 1931, he later lived there for two years (1934–1936), made friends among the best writers, and enjoyed an unusual success.

His first volume of poetry was *Perito en lunas* (An Expert in Moons) (1933), of a rather elaborate Gongoristic style; this was followed by several others, of which *El rayo que no cesa* (The Ceaseless Thunderbolt) (1936) is his best. In it Hernández shows a mastery of poetical diction and sounds a fully tragic note as he contemplates his destiny, torn as he is between love for his wife and family and feelings of powerlessness in the face of cruel forces of fate.

The poem included here belongs to a later book, *El hombre acecha* (Man Is Lurking, *or* Man on the Lookout) (1939), only partially published during the poet's lifetime. It is a desolate book, full of the horror of war and prison, of hunger and tortures, of hospitals and wounded men, such as the men in this train, moving in the night, unendingly. Hernandez's is a cruel, realistic, virile poetry, which has had a strong influence on the younger generation of Spanish poets.

El tren de los heridos

Silencio que naufraga en el silencio
de las bocas cerradas por la noche.
No cesa de callar ni atravesarlo.
Habla el lenguaje ahogado de los muertos.
Silencio.

Abre caminos de algodón profundo,
amordaza las ruedas de los relojes,
detén la voz del mar, de la paloma:
emociona la noche de los sueños.
Silencio.

El tren lluvioso de la sangre suelta,
el frágil tren de los que se desangran,
el silencioso, el doloroso, el pálido,
el tren callado de los sufrimientos.
Silencio.

Tren de la palidez mortal que asciende:
la palidez reviste las cabezas,
el ¡ay! la voz, el corazón, la tierra,
el corazón de los que malhirieron.
Silencio.

Van derramando piernas, brazos, ojos,
van derramando por el tren pedazos.
Pasan dejando rastros de amargura,
otra vía láctea de estelares miembros.
Silencio.

Ronco tren desmayado, enrojecido:
agoniza el carbón, suspira el humo,
y maternal la máquina suspira,
avanza como un largo desaliento.
Silencio.

The Train of the Wounded

Silence shipwrecked in the silence
of the mouths closed at night.
It does not cease to be silent or to traverse it.
It speaks the drowned language of the dead.
Silence.

It opens roads of deep cotton,
gags the wheels of the watches,
stops the voice of the ocean, of the dove:
it stirs with emotion the night of dreams.
Silence.

The rainy train of flowing blood,
the fragile train of the bleeding,
the silent, painful, pallid train,
the hushed train of suffering.
Silence.

Train of the mounting mortal pallor:
the pallor coating the heads,
the cry of pain, the voice, the heart, the ground,
the hearts of the badly wounded.
Silence.

They are spilling out legs, arms, eyes—
they are spilling out fragments all over the train.
They pass, leaving a wake of bitterness,
a second Milky Way of starry limbs.
Silence.

A hoarse, faltering, reddened train:
the coal is dying, the smoke sighs,
and the engine sighs like a mother
and pushes forward like a long dejection.
Silence.

Detenerse quisiera bajo un túnel
la larga madre, sollozar tendida.
No hay estaciones donde detenerse,
si no es el hospital, si no es el pecho.

Para vivir, con un pedazo basta:
en un rincón de carne cabe un hombre.
Un dedo sólo, un trozo sólo de ala
alza el vuelo total de todo el cuerpo.
Silencio.

Detened ese tren agonizante
que nunca acaba de cruzar la noche.

Y se queda descalzo hasta el caballo,
y enarena los cascos y el aliento.

This long mother would like to stop
in a tunnel and lie down to sob.
There are no stations to stop at,
except in the hospital or the heart.

To live, a fragment is enough:
a man can squeeze into a corner of flesh.
A single finger, a single piece of wing
can support the total flight of the entire body.
Silence.

Stop that dying train
that never ceases to cross the night.

And even the horse remains unshod,
and sand gets into its hoofs and breath.

Picture Sources and Credits

MARQUÉS DE SANTILLANA (p. 18) and GARCILASO DE LA VEGA (p. 36). From *Retratos de los españoles ilustres*. Madrid, 1791. In the library of the Hispanic Society of America.

GUTIERRE DE CETINA (p. 40), FRAY LUIS DE LEÓN (p. 44) and SAN JUAN DE LA CRUZ (p. 50). From Pacheco, Francisco: *Libro de descripción de verdaderos retratos* . . . . Sevilla, 1599. In the library of the Hispanic Society of America.

LUIS DE GÓNGORA Y ARGOTE (p. 56). From *Todas las obras*. Madrid, 1633. In the library of the Hispanic Society of America.

MIGUEL DE UNAMUNO (p. 86). From Torrente Ballester, Gonzalo: *Panorama de la literatura española contemporánea*. Madrid, 1961. Courtesy of Ediciones Guadarrama, Madrid. Photograph by Alfonso, Madrid.

ANTONIO MACHADO (p. 90). Photograph of a painting by Joaquín Sorolla y Bastida. Courtesy of the Hispanic Society of America.

PEDRO SALINAS (p. 102). Photo by Chamudes.

FREDERICO GARCÍA LORCA (p. 110). From Torrente Ballester, Gonzalo: *Panorama de la literatura española contemporánea*. Madrid, 1961. Courtesy of Ediciones Guadarrama, Madrid.

DÁMASO ALONSO (p. 116). From Torrente Ballester, Gonzalo: *Panorama de la literatura española contemporánea*. Madrid, 1961. Courtesy of Ediciones Guadarrama, Madrid. Photograph by Estudio Lagos, Madrid.

EMILIO PRADOS (p. 120). Courtesy of Cuadernos Americanos, Mexico City.

RAFAEL ALBERTI (p. 128). From Torrente Ballester, Gonzalo: *Panorama de la literatura española contemporánea*. Madrid, 1961. Courtesy of Ediciones Guadarrama, Madrid. Photograph by Alfonso, Madrid.

LUIS CERNUDA (p. 132). From Torrente Ballester, Gonzalo: *Panorama de la literatura española contemporánea*. Madrid, 1961. Courtesy of Ediciones Guadarrama, Madrid.

MIGUEL HERNÁNDEZ (p. 136). Courtesy of Editorial Losada, Buenos Aires.

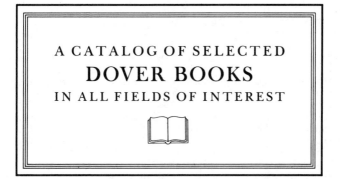

A CATALOG OF SELECTED
DOVER BOOKS
IN ALL FIELDS OF INTEREST

A CATALOG OF SELECTED DOVER
BOOKS IN ALL FIELDS OF INTEREST

CONCERNING THE SPIRITUAL IN ART, Wassily Kandinsky. Pioneering work by father of abstract art. Thoughts on color theory, nature of art. Analysis of earlier masters. 12 illustrations. 80pp. of text. 5⅜ x 8½.　　　　　　23411-8 Pa. $4.95

ANIMALS: 1,419 Copyright-Free Illustrations of Mammals, Birds, Fish, Insects, etc., Jim Harter (ed.). Clear wood engravings present, in extremely lifelike poses, over 1,000 species of animals. One of the most extensive pictorial sourcebooks of its kind. Captions. Index. 284pp. 9 x 12.　　　　　　23766-4 Pa. $14.95

CELTIC ART: The Methods of Construction, George Bain. Simple geometric techniques for making Celtic interlacements, spirals, Kells-type initials, animals, humans, etc. Over 500 illustrations. 160pp. 9 x 12. (USO)　　　　　　22923-8 Pa. $9.95

AN ATLAS OF ANATOMY FOR ARTISTS, Fritz Schider. Most thorough reference work on art anatomy in the world. Hundreds of illustrations, including selections from works by Vesalius, Leonardo, Goya, Ingres, Michelangelo, others. 593 illustrations. 192pp. 7⅛ x 10¼.　　　　　　20241-0 Pa. $9.95

CELTIC HAND STROKE-BY-STROKE (Irish Half-Uncial from "The Book of Kells"): An Arthur Baker Calligraphy Manual, Arthur Baker. Complete guide to creating each letter of the alphabet in distinctive Celtic manner. Covers hand position, strokes, pens, inks, paper, more. Illustrated. 48pp. 8¼ x 11.　　　24336-2 Pa. $3.95

EASY ORIGAMI, John Montroll. Charming collection of 32 projects (hat, cup, pelican, piano, swan, many more) specially designed for the novice origami hobbyist. Clearly illustrated easy-to-follow instructions insure that even beginning papercrafters will achieve successful results. 48pp. 8¼ x 11.　　　27298-2 Pa. $3.50

THE COMPLETE BOOK OF BIRDHOUSE CONSTRUCTION FOR WOOD-WORKERS, Scott D. Campbell. Detailed instructions, illustrations, tables. Also data on bird habitat and instinct patterns. Bibliography. 3 tables. 63 illustrations in 15 figures. 48pp. 5¼ x 8½.　　　　　　24407-5 Pa. $2.50

BLOOMINGDALE'S ILLUSTRATED 1886 CATALOG: Fashions, Dry Goods and Housewares, Bloomingdale Brothers. Famed merchants' extremely rare catalog depicting about 1,700 products: clothing, housewares, firearms, dry goods, jewelry, more. Invaluable for dating, identifying vintage items. Also, copyright-free graphics for artists, designers. Co-published with Henry Ford Museum & Greenfield Village. 160pp. 8¼ x 11.　　　　　　25780-0 Pa. $10.95

HISTORIC COSTUME IN PICTURES, Braun & Schneider. Over 1,450 costumed figures in clearly detailed engravings–from dawn of civilization to end of 19th century. Captions. Many folk costumes. 256pp. 8⅜ x 11¾.　　　23150-X Pa. $12.95

STICKLEY CRAFTSMAN FURNITURE CATALOGS, Gustav Stickley and L. & J. G. Stickley. Beautiful, functional furniture in two authentic catalogs from 1910. 594 illustrations, including 277 photos, show settles, rockers, armchairs, reclining chairs, bookcases, desks, tables. 183pp. 6½ x 9¼.   23838-5 Pa. $11.95

AMERICAN LOCOMOTIVES IN HISTORIC PHOTOGRAPHS: 1858 to 1949, Ron Ziel (ed.). A rare collection of 126 meticulously detailed official photographs, called "builder portraits," of American locomotives that majestically chronicle the rise of steam locomotive power in America. Introduction. Detailed captions. xi + 129pp. 9 x 12.   27393-8 Pa. $13.95

AMERICA'S LIGHTHOUSES: An Illustrated History, Francis Ross Holland, Jr. Delightfully written, profusely illustrated fact-filled survey of over 200 American light-houses since 1716. History, anecdotes, technological advances, more. 240pp. 8 x 10¾.
25576-X Pa. $12.95

TOWARDS A NEW ARCHITECTURE, Le Corbusier. Pioneering manifesto by founder of "International School." Technical and aesthetic theories, views of indus-try, economics, relation of form to function, "mass-production split" and much more. Profusely illustrated. 320pp. 6⅛ x 9¼. (USO)   25023-7 Pa. $9.95

HOW THE OTHER HALF LIVES, Jacob Riis. Famous journalistic record, expos-ing poverty and degradation of New York slums around 1900, by major social reformer. 100 striking and influential photographs. 233pp. 10 x 7⅞.
22012-5 Pa. $11.95

FRUIT KEY AND TWIG KEY TO TREES AND SHRUBS, William M. Harlow. One of the handiest and most widely used identification aids. Fruit key covers 120 deciduous and evergreen species; twig key 160 deciduous species. Easily used. Over 300 photographs. 126pp. 5⅜ x 8½.   20511-8 Pa. $3.95

COMMON BIRD SONGS, Dr. Donald J. Borror. Songs of 60 most common U.S. birds: robins, sparrows, cardinals, bluejays, finches, more—arranged in order of increasing complexity. Up to 9 variations of songs of each species.
Cassette and manual 99911-4 $8.95

ORCHIDS AS HOUSE PLANTS, Rebecca Tyson Northen. Grow cattleyas and many other kinds of orchids—in a window, in a case, or under artificial light. 63 illus-trations. 148pp. 5⅜ x 8½.   23261-1 Pa. $5.95

MONSTER MAZES, Dave Phillips. Masterful mazes at four levels of difficulty. Avoid deadly perils and evil creatures to find magical treasures. Solutions for all 32 exciting illustrated puzzles. 48pp. 8¼ x 11.   26005-4 Pa. $2.95

MOZART'S DON GIOVANNI (DOVER OPERA LIBRETTO SERIES), Wolfgang Amadeus Mozart. Introduced and translated by Ellen H. Bleiler. Standard Italian libretto, with complete English translation. Convenient and thoroughly portable—an ideal companion for reading along with a recording or the performance itself. Introduction. List of characters. Plot summary. 121pp. 5¼ x 8½.
24944-1 Pa. $3.95

TECHNICAL MANUAL AND DICTIONARY OF CLASSICAL BALLET, Gail Grant. Defines, explains, comments on steps, movements, poses and concepts. 15-page pictorial section. Basic book for student, viewer. 127pp. 5⅜ x 8½.
21843-0 Pa. $4.95

BRASS INSTRUMENTS: Their History and Development, Anthony Baines. Authoritative, updated survey of the evolution of trumpets, trombones, bugles, cornets, French horns, tubas and other brass wind instruments. Over 140 illustrations and 48 music examples. Corrected and updated by author. New preface. Bibliography. 320pp. 5⅜ x 8½. 27574-4 Pa. $9.95

HOLLYWOOD GLAMOR PORTRAITS, John Kobal (ed.). 145 photos from 1926-49. Harlow, Gable, Bogart, Bacall; 94 stars in all. Full background on photographers, technical aspects. 160pp. 8⅜ x 11¼. 23352-9 Pa. $12.95

MAX AND MORITZ, Wilhelm Busch. Great humor classic in both German and English. Also 10 other works: "Cat and Mouse," "Plisch and Plumm," etc. 216pp. 5⅜ x 8½. 20181-3 Pa. $6.95

THE RAVEN AND OTHER FAVORITE POEMS, Edgar Allan Poe. Over 40 of the author's most memorable poems: "The Bells," "Ulalume," "Israfel," "To Helen," "The Conqueror Worm," "Eldorado," "Annabel Lee," many more. Alphabetic lists of titles and first lines. 64pp. 5³⁄₁₆ x 8¼. 26685-0 Pa. $1.00

PERSONAL MEMOIRS OF U. S. GRANT, Ulysses Simpson Grant. Intelligent, deeply moving firsthand account of Civil War campaigns, considered by many the finest military memoirs ever written. Includes letters, historic photographs, maps and more. 528pp. 6⅛ x 9¼. 28587-1 Pa. $12.95

AMULETS AND SUPERSTITIONS, E. A. Wallis Budge. Comprehensive discourse on origin, powers of amulets in many ancient cultures: Arab, Persian Babylonian, Assyrian, Egyptian, Gnostic, Hebrew, Phoenician, Syriac, etc. Covers cross, swastika, crucifix, seals, rings, stones, etc. 584pp. 5⅜ x 8½. 23573-4 Pa. $15.95

RUSSIAN STORIES/PYCCKNE PACCKA3bl: A Dual-Language Book, edited by Gleb Struve. Twelve tales by such masters as Chekhov, Tolstoy, Dostoevsky, Pushkin, others. Excellent word-for-word English translations on facing pages, plus teaching and study aids, Russian/English vocabulary, biographical/critical introductions, more. 416pp. 5⅜ x 8½. 26244-8 Pa. $9.95

PHILADELPHIA THEN AND NOW: 60 Sites Photographed in the Past and Present, Kenneth Finkel and Susan Oyama. Rare photographs of City Hall, Logan Square, Independence Hall, Betsy Ross House, other landmarks juxtaposed with contemporary views. Captures changing face of historic city. Introduction. Captions. 128pp. 8¼ x 11. 25790-8 Pa. $9.95

AIA ARCHITECTURAL GUIDE TO NASSAU AND SUFFOLK COUNTIES, LONG ISLAND, The American Institute of Architects, Long Island Chapter, and the Society for the Preservation of Long Island Antiquities. Comprehensive, well-researched and generously illustrated volume brings to life over three centuries of Long Island's great architectural heritage. More than 240 photographs with authoritative, extensively detailed captions. 176pp. 8¼ x 11. 26946-9 Pa. $14.95

NORTH AMERICAN INDIAN LIFE: Customs and Traditions of 23 Tribes, Elsie Clews Parsons (ed.). 27 fictionalized essays by noted anthropologists examine religion, customs, government, additional facets of life among the Winnebago, Crow, Zuni, Eskimo, other tribes. 480pp. 6⅛ x 9¼. 27377-6 Pa. $10.95

CATALOG OF DOVER BOOKS

THE INFLUENCE OF SEA POWER UPON HISTORY, 1660–1783, A. T. Mahan. Influential classic of naval history and tactics still used as text in war colleges. First paperback edition. 4 maps. 24 battle plans. 640pp. 5⅜ x 8½. 25509-3 Pa. $14.95

THE STORY OF THE TITANIC AS TOLD BY ITS SURVIVORS, Jack Winocour (ed.). What it was really like. Panic, despair, shocking inefficiency, and a little heroism. More thrilling than any fictional account. 26 illustrations. 320pp. 5⅜ x 8½. 20610-6 Pa. $8.95

FAIRY AND FOLK TALES OF THE IRISH PEASANTRY, William Butler Yeats (ed.). Treasury of 64 tales from the twilight world of Celtic myth and legend: "The Soul Cages," "The Kildare Pooka," "King O'Toole and his Goose," many more. Introduction and Notes by W. B. Yeats. 352pp. 5⅜ x 8½. 26941-8 Pa. $8.95

BUDDHIST MAHAYANA TEXTS, E. B. Cowell and Others (eds.). Superb, accurate translations of basic documents in Mahayana Buddhism, highly important in history of religions. The Buddha-karita of Asvaghosha, Larger Sukhavativyuha, more. 448pp. 5⅜ x 8½. 25552-2 Pa. $12.95

ONE TWO THREE . . . INFINITY: Facts and Speculations of Science, George Gamow. Great physicist's fascinating, readable overview of contemporary science: number theory, relativity, fourth dimension, entropy, genes, atomic structure, much more. 128 illustrations. Index. 352pp. 5⅜ x 8½. 25664-2 Pa. $8.95

ENGINEERING IN HISTORY, Richard Shelton Kirby, et al. Broad, nontechnical survey of history's major technological advances: birth of Greek science, industrial revolution, electricity and applied science, 20th-century automation, much more. 181 illustrations. ". . . excellent . . ."–Isis. Bibliography. vii + 530pp. 5⅜ x 8¼. 26412-2 Pa. $14.95

DALÍ ON MODERN ART: The Cuckolds of Antiquated Modern Art, Salvador Dalí. Influential painter skewers modern art and its practitioners. Outrageous evaluations of Picasso, Cézanne, Turner, more. 15 renderings of paintings discussed. 44 calligraphic decorations by Dalí. 96pp. 5⅜ x 8½. (USO) 29220-7 Pa. $4.95

ANTIQUE PLAYING CARDS: A Pictorial History, Henry René D'Allemagne. Over 900 elaborate, decorative images from rare playing cards (14th–20th centuries): Bacchus, death, dancing dogs, hunting scenes, royal coats of arms, players cheating, much more. 96pp. 9¼ x 12¼. 29265-7 Pa. $12.95

MAKING FURNITURE MASTERPIECES: 30 Projects with Measured Drawings, Franklin H. Gottshall. Step-by-step instructions, illustrations for constructing handsome, useful pieces, among them a Sheraton desk, Chippendale chair, Spanish desk, Queen Anne table and a William and Mary dressing mirror. 224pp. 8⅛ x 11¼. 29338-6 Pa. $13.95

THE FOSSIL BOOK: A Record of Prehistoric Life, Patricia V. Rich et al. Profusely illustrated definitive guide covers everything from single-celled organisms and dinosaurs to birds and mammals and the interplay between climate and man. Over 1,500 illustrations. 760pp. 7½ x 10⅛. 29371-8 Pa. $29.95

Prices subject to change without notice.

Available at your book dealer or write for free catalog to Dept. GI, Dover Publications, Inc., 31 East 2nd St., Mineola, N.Y. 11501. Dover publishes more than 500 books each year on science, elementary and advanced mathematics, biology, music, art, literary history, social sciences and other areas.